T0417793

Changing Assessment

IBE on Curriculum, Learning, and Assessment

The titles published in this series are listed at *brill.com/ibe*

Changing Assessment

How to Design Curriculum for Human Flourishing

By

Conrad Hughes

BRILL

LEIDEN | BOSTON

All chapters in this book have undergone peer review.

The Library of Congress Cataloging-in-Publication Data is available online at https://catalog.loc.gov

Typeface for the Latin, Greek, and Cyrillic scripts: "Brill". See and download: brill.com/brill-typeface.

ISSN 2772-4549
ISBN 978-90-04-71418-2 (paperback)
ISBN 978-90-04-71419-9 (hardback)
ISBN 978-90-04-71420-5 (e-book)
DOI 10.1163/9789004714205

This book is printed on acid-free paper and produced in a sustainable manner.

This book is dedicated to my wife, Estelle Baroung Hughes.

∵

Contents

Foreword

Changing Assessment: How to Design Curriculum for Human Flourishing is a necessary contribution to the ongoing discussion on curriculum relevance and inclusivity, a topic central to the International Bureau of Education (IBE)'s mission and global education transformation efforts. The book addresses a pressing question in today's fast-changing world: How can schools design assessments that capture the necessary skills, attitudes, and knowledge required for contributing to individual, collective, and public good?

This succinct, well-researched, and compelling book by Conrad Hughes focuses on assessments with a summative purpose at the end of secondary schooling. Hughes argues that it is at this point that the pressure of assessment is at its strongest, making it a critical area for educational stakeholders to reform.

Why such reform? End-of-secondary-school assessments are often too narrow, high stakes, and fail to account for the diverse talents young people bring to the world. Competencies such as creativity and collaboration, which are increasingly sought in the 21st century, are not adequately reflected in most traditional examination-based assessments.

Conrad Hughes provides an overview of the history of the development of assessments, highlighting the complexities, challenges, and opportunities they present in the field of education. He critically examines the current state of school assessments by delving into the sociological and ideological roots of 19th-century models, revealing their lasting impact on contemporary education. The organisation of timetables, grading systems, and large-scale assessments are discussed, alongside the struggles these systems faced during the Covid-19 pandemic. This section underscores the high-pressure relationship between university admissions and end of secondary schooling, shedding light on the inherent limitations of the prevailing assessment model.

Building upon this analysis, Hughes explores a range of alternative assessment models. From innovative practices in primary and middle schools to creative and transdisciplinary university courses, and even assessment methods in the workplace, he showcases the diversity and potential of approaches that move beyond traditional examination frameworks. This exploration highlights how assessment practices can evolve to better reflect the multifaceted talents of students.

Over the past decades, UNESCO IBE has supported numerous countries and institutions in competency-based curriculum reforms, of which assessment reform is an integral part. The book culminates with a compelling case study that highlights UNESCO IBE's work on global competencies and its implementation at the International School of Geneva under Dr. Hughes' leadership. This case study exemplifies the type of reform needed to foster a more holistic appreciation of student learning and provides an innovative blueprint for transforming learning assessment.

Changing Assessment: How to Design Curriculum for Human Flourishing is a must-read for all those involved in curriculum design and assessment. It offers a critical analysis of current assessment practices and presents a vision for reform that aligns with UNESCO IBE's goals of promoting inclusive, equitable, and quality education for all. This book not only highlights significant drawbacks in existing practices but also serves as a call to action for celebrating human flourishing through more comprehensive and reflective assessment systems.

Svein Osttveit
UNESCO IBE Director a.i.

CHAPTER 1

The Problem with Schools Today

1   Human Intelligence Is Not a Single, Narrow Construct

What is the purpose of school? The simple answer: to educate students so that they are prepared for the world. There are many different ways communities can do this, of course, which is why there are so many different types of schools. However, when one scours the horizon of twenty-first-century schools, one sees a high degree of commonality in that they all have a curriculum — a course of study with a syllabus, planned lessons, and assessments.

The assessment system should be formative — that is, designed to help learning — but it is the summative function of assessment as a judgement of student work that gives it its central importance in schooling from the perspective of students. The summative assessment system is essentially built to valorise students who are successful in their journey through the curriculum. This assessment tends to be done at the end of assignments through a grading system whereby excellent performance is awarded a high grade; average performance, a medium grade; and poor performance, a low grade. The implications of this sorting mechanism are not trivial: as we all know, low grades can ultimately mean not receiving an end-of-year qualification. If this happens, opportunities for integration in the world of work are low and future prospects, limited.[1] On the other hand, those who achieve high grades will have a higher chance of accessing future educational opportunities (tertiary education places, bursaries, and internships) and creating wealth (Biasi et al., 2021).

The idea that success in the educational sector predicts broader social and economic success is called human capital theory (Becker, 1975): "[I]nvestment in education makes individuals more productive, and it is this that results in higher wages. Individuals invest in education if the benefits in the form of increased earnings over their lifetime exceed the costs" (Wyness et al., 2021, p. 2).[2]

This theory can be contrasted with signalling theory (Spence, 1974), which proposes that human capital is not actually developed substantively through a formal education system; instead, graduates aim for certificates and diplomas because these tell employers that the graduates are worthwhile investments since they have succeeded in the world of institutional certification. In other words, when students graduate, they are showing the world what they have done rather than investing in their potential to do more.

Whether education develops human capital or is merely a signal of past achievements, or both, this schooling system is meant to be based on meritocratic principles whereby those who are talented and work hard will be rewarded. In later sections of this book, we will see that it is naive to think that the grading system is entirely meritocratic as, in reality, it describes social advantage as much as raw talent: the two become difficult to disentangle since those who do well on school tests tend to come from educated backgrounds in the first place. However, given that there are still many stories of children from poor and uneducated backgrounds ("uneducated" in the sense that parents will be unqualified) who go very far in the formal testing contexts of schools, one can argue that there are opportunities, at least, for those who are particularly determined and motivated to do well and, therefore, to succeed. In fact, this idea is very important as it drives an entire belief in education as a motor for social renewal through individual, collective, and public flourishing, opportunity, and development.[3]

However, the central question — irrespective of whether grading systems are fair in their technical or sociological underpinning structure — is, what exactly is being tested? or, as we would phrase it in the science of assessment, what is the construct (Jamieson, 2013)?

Since at least the Middle Ages, the construct that has overwhelmingly dominated educational assessment has been academic knowledge: what you know about subjects. This in itself is no bad thing: knowing basic arithmetic, literacy, science, the arts, and humanities equips young people with cultural references that will help them function in society, have opinions, and communicate with other people who draw from a similar bank of knowledge. For human beings to work together, there must be some modicum of commonality within their communications system: language, semiotics, understanding of historical facts, and acknowledgement of laws both scientific and social (Cole et al., 1978). As such, the construct of academic knowledge is central in the important thrust of cultural transmission that characterises education and schooling.

Knowledge makes itself known in human beings through cultural practices. These are, fundamentally, song, dance, visual arts, speaking, and writing. These cultural practices create a mental product, which might be a story, a manuscript, a theory, an observation, an action, or an artistic composition. For these cultural practices to develop, skill is needed. Skills are the embodiment of knowledge, the capabilities necessary to appropriate knowledge, to shape it and to create it.

Thus, closely connected to the construct of knowledge — in fact, inseparable from it and inextricably woven into the very fabric and incarnation of knowledge — is skill. For example, when you learn to play a musical instrument, you are learning technical, physical skills necessary to produce sound from the instrument but also what the notes are and how they work together, the theory of music, as it were. When you learn how to paint, you learn how to use the brush, how to mix paints, and different painting techniques, but you also learn the rules of composition, what colours are, what conditions allow paint to dry in a certain way, and so on.

Theory and application are often separated: we may learn the theory of composition or what the primary colours are in a separate, abstract, and nonphysical environment, through language and understanding. Then, we will apply this learning in a technical exercise, which is playing the instrument or painting. Theoretical or active approaches to learning create different pedagogical schools of thought: some teachers prefer to spend a lot of time explaining the theory of chemistry, others wish to have students learn the theory through application. This goes so far as to lead to subdivisions in the way subjects are presented: pure maths and applied maths; drama and theatre; theoretical physics and experimental physics.

The problem with assessment in schools is not that it is focussed on the construct of academic knowledge and the skills associated with academic knowledge; the problem is that it is essentially *only* focussed on the construct of academic knowledge and those skills specifically associated with academic knowledge (Hughes, 2023). Students who do well in school can perform well on tests and fieldwork exercises associated with academics: multiple-choice tests in science, essays in history, oral commentaries on literature, short-item responses in a second language, written or oral responses to economic problems (showing an understanding of economic theory), performance or composition of a piece of music (evincing an understanding of the rules of composition, harmony, rhythm, and melody).

One more important dimension of what is tested is the ability to prepare for a test and to take the test with a calm mind and controlled nerves. This is often overlooked in curriculum design, where the focus is on the syllabus and the academic skills learnt through the syllabus in the classroom. However, it is not only that knowledge and those skills that are solicited during test taking but also a psychological state: in brief, the ability to perform under pressure. Anyone who has taken an examination realizes that equally important to having mastered the subjects on the examination and having learned the skills to answer the questions is the state of mind and concentration needed to think clearly while taking exams.[4]

If the field of knowledge that is emphasised in schools is academic knowledge and the skills that are valued are academic skills, *the superordinate, recurring state of mind that is emphasised is test-taking ability.*

So, what happens to the students who are not good at writing commentaries or answering multiple-choice tests? What happens to the students who freeze up when put in front of a timed exercise? What happens to the students who never manage to express themselves clearly in writing or orally? What happens to the students who struggle to understand and memorise academic concepts? What will be the fate of students who are not drawn to books, whiteboard notes, lectures, and the specific, intellectual world of schooling?

In the current education system, at least in the vast majority of school systems, these students fail or drop out. There are two ways of considering these students: either they can be considered as not good at school — or we could say school was not good to them.

The difference between these two postulates is important. The first one is built on the assumptions that the educational model is a fair measure of intrinsic potential and that the norm is to graduate. Students who are not successful at school carry stigma with them: "high school dropouts", "uneducated", "unqualified", "unskilled", they "failed" or "did not pass" — and very often parents and families are ashamed of their children when this happens. The second postulate places the responsibility less on the individual and more on the structure: it is based on the assumptions that every human being has potential in some area and that schools should be able to bring out that potential, make it flourish, and recognise it.

It is this book's contention that knowledge and skill stretch across a much broader canvas than the traditional, narrow academic pathway that constricts learning in high school. As I progress with my argument, I will show several aspects to this argument, which run from the narrowness of the curriculum, the prevalence of certain subjects in the curriculum, ignored extracurricular and home activities, human competences that are extremely important for human flourishing and success in the broader sense of the term but are not recognised in formal assessments — all the way through to the devastating implications this paradigm has for the world of work, social organisation, and even the future of our planet.

The situation has become chronic; the end-of-school assessment must change.

2   Human Beings Possess a Wealth of Experiences and Gifts but Few of Them Are Recognised in Formal Assessment Systems

Observing human behaviour with an open mind tells a story. Each individual behaves in a social context that might or might not bring out her/his/their strongest qualities. For example, if you are sitting in a restaurant and watching different waiters serve the food, before long you will notice that some are quicker, more confident, and more engaged than others. This could be for a host of reasons: some are more experienced than others; some might be having a bad day, whereas others might be particularly motivated. Finally, some will be able to adapt to the skill set required to be a waiter more fluently than others: they appear to be better suited to the job.

For society to thrive and for individuals in that society to thrive, each individual's energy, passion, and motivation to do work should correspond to the work itself. A dream world would be one where everybody was engaged in some form of work that suited them.

While this idea might seem utopian and unrealistic, it is a dream we should hold on to; and it is precisely with this dream in mind that we should modify the model of end-of-school assessment. Further still, *it is by modifying the assessment structures at the school level that such a scenario — where talent could truly thrive — might be made possible in the marketplace and in societies at large.*

In short, if a child loves sport, they should not be punished through a one-size-fits-all academic-curriculum straitjacket that pushes them away from sports. On the contrary, such children should be given an opportunity to develop their interest in sports. If a child loves theatre and music, they should not be placed before a curriculum framework where these subjects are presented as less important than other subjects, such as science and mathematics. We are looking at deep questions of agency, expression, competence development, and, ultimately, freedom.

If a child develops a project outside of school, school should show interest in that project and arrange the curriculum in such a way that this can feature in the child's learning. If a mentor sees a particular gift in a student, the learning environment placed around the student should allow that gift to grow, to flourish.

While these ideas might seem difficult, if not impossible, to operationalise in the senior years of high school — currently so crowded out by examinations — it is already being done in some schools and it can be done at a much larger scale. It is a question of courage and coordination: these two forces can and must bring about the reform needed to escape the current summative assessment chokehold.

2.1 Schools Are Designed around the End-of-High-School Assessment Model

The nerve point of the assessment model is the end of high school (also called secondary school). The ramifications stretch outward into the world of higher-education and post-high school employment opportunities, and downward into the rungs of lower high school and, in some systems (like in the English national curriculum), all the way down to middle school. (See the "11 plus" examination system in Allen & Bartley, 2017.) This is for the simple reason that the end-of-high-school qualification is high stakes: it is seen and treated as more than a set of examinations — these are tests that will define a student's probability of socioeconomic integration and success. This means that students, parents, and teachers, in a state of fear more than anything else, adapt their behaviours considerably to accommodate these end-of-school examinations.

Teachers teach to the test: educational authorities judge pre–high school curricula according to the extent to which they prepare students for the end game of terminal examinations. Universities, particularly private and selective universities, place enormous pressure on test takers, examination boards, and schools to obtain strong results. League tables drive results-oriented behaviour and increase the appetite for selectivity: some high schools become afraid of failure because prospective parents will look to their results as a gauge of quality and therefore do not wish to give too many of their students the chance even to sit the examinations so as to preserve results.

If this juggernaut is dismantled, the entire ecosystem of high school would change for the better.

This is not to say that academics and tough assessments should not have their part to play in an education or that there is no room for selectivity. It is the valency, the predominance, and the extremity of this model that need to be modified so that the student experience at the end of high school is more balanced, more serene, and, most especially, more inclusive, allowing for students to showcase and society to celebrate several types of intelligence and talent.

2.2   *This Assessment System Kills Creativity in Students and Teachers*

From the 1980s to the early 2000s, Kyung Hee Kim, professor of education at William and Mary College, conducted research on creativity in over 300 000 school children. Using the Tests of Creative Thinking (Torrance, 1990), he found a decline in creativity over time (2011). More specifically,

> Children's ability to produce unique and unusual ideas (Originality) increased up to fifth grade [but] decreased through high school ... [and their] ability to be intellectually curious and to be open-minded (Resistance to Premature Closure) followed a similar path. (Kim, 2011, p. 291)

It's a fascinating study that shows an overall decline in creative thinking, including in the early years. Jean Piaget thought that children's ability to develop abstract thought and more intertwined, complex ideas would increase with time — which suggests that, if Piaget's theory was correct, the effect of social forces on what should be an upward trend in creative thinking must be very strong.

In a heartrending article published in *Varsity* (an independent newspaper for the University of Cambridge), Miranda Stephenson (2020) comments on the British system of high schooling:

> [T]here's not just a government pressure to pass exams, but also an overbearing pressure to pass the right exams. In just the same way that hobbies are neglected in favour of set, personal-statement-boosting supra-curricular activities, a diverse range of subjects are increasingly devalued in favour of those deemed most "facilitating". As a humanities student, I had been asked to consider Maths for A-Level; as a STEM student, my sister was told to take extra Physics instead of Art. No matter how many vague platitudes my secondary school spewed, the dominant emphasis was never on creative thinking or independence of choice, but on a subject's supposed "utility".

The best-known criticism of the schooling system concerning creativity is Ken Robinson's 2006 TED Talk *Do Schools Kill Creativity?*, which, at the time of this writing, has grossed over 76 million views (Robinson, 2006). In it, Robinson blames the assessment system's vilification of mistakes as core to the demise of creativity in schools. Nowhere is this tendency stronger than in the form of high-pressure examinations at the end of high school, where each mistake can cost students points that will ultimately determine their grade — and their future. Robinson (2006) points out that

> the whole system of public education around the world is a protracted process of university entrance. And the consequence is that many highly-talented, brilliant, creative people think they're not, because the thing they were good at at school wasn't valued, or was actually stigmatized.

This is why changing the assessment system at the end of high school will affect the whole schooling system in a deep and structural manner, most especially if we rethink the pressure on students to perform on a narrow set of skills.

2.3 *Appearance Can Be Deceiving: The Present Assessment Paradigm Is More Plutocratic Than Meritocratic*

One argument that can be made in favour of the status quo is that it is meritocratic. The argument goes: The current system might be stressful and difficult, and not everybody's strengths will necessarily be matched perfectly in all academic subjects, but at least the assessment system is fair in that everybody is treated equally and those that muster enough effort in studying and preparing have the opportunity to succeed. However, this is not entirely true.

Numerous studies have shown that academic success is predicated upon social advantage.[5]

Chetty, Deming, and Friedman (2023) show that, in the United States, "children from families in the top 1% are twice as likely to attend an Ivy-Plus college ... as those from middle-class families with comparable SAT/ACT scores". Dräger found that, in Germany, "children living in wealthy households are 20 percent more likely to attend the highest track in fifth grade and to obtain the highest school-leaving certificate" (2022).

This is because children whose parents are well educated are more familiar with the world of academic testing. Furthermore, wealthy parents can afford extra tuition and coaching if their children fall behind. Some argue that the advantage students have in the present assessment system extends beyond grades to questions of race (Justice, 2023) and gender (Pyne, 2020).

3   A Problem That Can Be Solved

The narrowing of assessment in high schools is not an insurmountable problem. For the curriculum to be broader and more inclusive, it must be adapted to the needs of students, and its structure requires more flexibility. As this book progresses, we will see how this is already being done in some contexts, and how it can be done in others.

If we achieve these reforms, we can make the future of education and the world of work more mindful and centred on human flourishing. The work is of utmost importance.

Notes

1   Ghignoni et al. (2019) show that university dropouts struggle to access the workplace compared to graduates. Rosenbaum (2001) shows that, in the United States, students graduating with Cs or lower have a much lower chance of earning college degrees.

2   For Wyness et al. (2021), "[T]here is a clear picture of substantial importance for human capital theory as a dominant part of the link between education and later earnings" (p. 1).

3   The UIS policy paper "Reducing global poverty through universal primary and secondary education" shows that basic reading skills among students in low-income countries would lead to almost 171 million people escaping extreme poverty (UIS, 2017).

4   For a detailed discussion on the challenges and pitfalls facing ecological validity, see Shamay-Tsoory & Mendelsohn (2019).
5   For an overview of these studies, see Hughes, 2021.

References

Allen, R., & Bartley J. (2017). The role of the eleven-plus test papers and appeals in producing social inequalities in access to grammar schools. *National Institute Economic Review, 240,* 30–41. https://doi.org/10.1177/002795011724000112

Becker, G. S. (1975). *Human capital: A theoretical and empirical analysis, with special reference to education* (2nd ed.), National Bureau of Economic Research.

Biasi, B., Deming, D. J., & Moser, P. (2021). *Education and innovation.* Working paper 28544. National Bureau of Economic Research.

Chetty, R., Deming, D. J., & Friedman, J. (2023). *Diversifying society's leaders? The determinants and causal effects of admission to highly selective private colleges.* Working paper 31492. National Bureau of Economic Research. https://opportunity-insights.org/paper/collegeadmissions/

Cole, M., John-Steiner, V., Scribner, S., & Souberman, E. (Eds.). (1978). *Mind in society: The development of higher psychological processes.* Harvard University Press.

Dräger, J. (2022). The role of parental wealth in children's educational pathways in Germany. *European Sociological Review, 38*(1), 18–36, https://doi.org/10.1093/esr/jcab027

Ghignoni, E., Croce, G., & d'Ambrosio, A. (2019). University dropouts vs high school graduates in the school-to-work transition: Who is doing better? *International Journal of Manpower, 40*(3), 449–472, https://doi.org/10.1108/IJM-02-2018-0051

Hughes, C. (2021). *Education and elitism: Challenges and opportunities.* Routledge.

Hughes, C. (2023). *The necessity to broaden assessment and how we can do it.* Curriculum on the Move thematic notes 18. UNESCO International Bureau of Education (IBE). https://unesdoc.unesco.org/ark:/48223/pf0000384874

Jamieson, J. (2013). Defining constructs and assessment design. In A. J. Kunnan (Ed.), *The companion to language assessment.* https://doi.org/10.1002/9781118411360.wbcla062

Justice, B. (2023). Schooling as a white good. *History of Education Quarterly, 63*(2), 154–178. https://doi.org/10.1017/heq.2023.7

Kyung Hee Kim (2011). The creativity crisis: The decrease in creative thinking scores on the Torrance Tests of Creative Thinking. *Creativity Research Journal, 23*(4), 285–295.

Pyne, J. (2020). *Boys enjoy educational advantages despite being less engaged in school than girls.* Brookings Institute. https://www.brookings.edu/articles/boys-enjoy-educational-advantages-despite-being-less-engaged-in-school-than-girls/

Robinson, K. (2006). *Do schools kill creativity?* [Video]. TED Talk. https://www.ted
.com/talks/sir_ken_robinson_do_schools_kill_creativity?language=en

Rosenbaum, J. E. (2001). *Beyond college for all*. Russell Sage.

Shamay-Tsoory, S. G., & Mendelsohn, A. (2019). Real-life neuroscience: An ecological approach to brain and behavior research. *Perspectives on Psychological Science*,
14(5), 841–859. https://doi.org/10.1177/1745691619856350

Spence, M. (1973). Job market signaling. *Quarterly Journal of Economics, 87*(3), 355–374.

Stephenson, M. (2020). How the British school system is killing creativity. *Varsity*.
https://www.varsity.co.uk/features/19779

Torrance, E. P. (1990). *Torrance tests of creative thinking*. Scholastic Testing Service.

UIS [UNESCO Institute of Statistics]. (2017). *Reducing global poverty through universal
primary and secondary education*. Policy paper 32/ Fact sheet 44.
https://uis.unesco.org/en/files/reducing-global-poverty-through-universal-
primary-secondary-education-pdf

Wyness, G., Macmillan, L., & Anders, J. (2021). *Does education raise people's productivity or does it just signal their existing ability?* Briefing note 12. Centre for Education
Policy, UCL Institute of Education.

CHAPTER 2

The Sociology, Ideology, and Perpetuation of 19th-Century Assessment Models

1   The Origins of IQ Testing: A Zero-Sum Game

At the core of the assessment system that dominates schools is the intelligence quotient (IQ) test. The structure and intention of the test lies at the centre of the general approach to success in schools and helps explain why we are lumbered with a system that is so narrow and rigid.

To understand the impact it has on educational principles today, it is worth going to the historical origin of IQ testing and the philosophy behind its original inception, and, more specifically, how this original purpose was quickly distorted to suit aims altogether different to what it was intended.

1.1   *The First Ideas*

IQ testing was first conceptualised in the nineteenth century by Francis Galton (Bulmer, 1999), who believed that differences in intelligence were hereditary and could be measured. This was part of Galton's overall *weltanschauung,* belonging to a vast enterprise that can be situated at least as far back as Ancient Greece, which we will look at in the next section of this chapter. However, in 1905 the psychologists Alfred Binet, Victor Henri, and Théodore Simon created the IQ test as we know it today, though it was calculated slightly differently when they first invented it.

Binet, a Parisian psychologist who had worked with Charcot at the Salpêtrière, had been studying intelligence testing for decades, trying to capture various facets of human intelligence in creative and expansive ways. He was concerned with "memory; [the] nature of memory images; imagination; attention; power of understanding, observing, defining and distinguishing; suggestibility; aesthetic feeling; moral sentiments; muscular force and force of will; and motor ability" (Nicholas et al., 2014).

While Binet's research was focussed primarily on elements of memory, his assistant, Vitor Henri, specialised in spatial awareness. Through various iterations of the test, these two constructs (memory and spatial reasoning) came to feature as the dominant pillars of IQ testing. Thus, today, when we speak of intelligence, unless referring to less-quoted studies of multiple or triarchic intelligence, we are usually referring to logico-mathematical reasoning and pattern recognition. Binet's and Henri's publications in the late 1800s were important contributions to psychology, influencing Sigmund Freud and, many years later, Solomon Asch (Nicolas et al., 2014), in their recognition and understanding that human memory is highly fallible. From these inroads into human psychology till the present, researchers and psychologists have considered memory as the most fundamental aspect of cognition, and it features strongly in all forms of cognitive and intellectual testing. This might partially explain the emphasis on memorisation in the summative end-of-high-school assessments to this day.

The advent of public schooling in France meant that many children would be introduced to a curriculum for which they had little background knowledge — and therefore they would have difficulty learning. Binet was commissioned to design a test that could screen for ability, since the practice at the time was for psychologists to label students who were not performing as suffering from some sort of pathological condition and to have them interned in asylums. Binet's test recategorised students as less cognitively fluent but not as suffering from an illness. Students with low scores could stay in school but would need more support. Hence, the test's initial purpose was honourable: to protect students. However, Binet expressed concern, even in these early days, that the test would be misused. He could see that, in the wrong hands, it could be used not to protect but to hurt.

The test was out of 30 and was adaptive. The scores were a calculation based on the age of the child; results would be presented in a mean distribution curve, meaning that levels of intelligence were not measured as absolutes but as relative to a cohort. The essential principle was that intelligence would be measured according to the "norm".

1.2   *IQ Testing Becomes a Widespread Societal Practice*

By 1910, after statisticians like Charles Spearman had studied the test and psychometricians at Stanford had revised it, the Stanford-Binet test was created, which was an improved version of Binet's. The psychologists William Stern and Lewis Terman simplified and standardised the manner in which scores would be calculated, creating the present-day "intelligence quotient" (Lamiell, 2003).

Stern, like Binet, was concerned about how IQ scores would be used. He recognised that there are many different ways of being intelligent and was worried that — now that the calculation could be made relatively easily — many would rush to draw hasty conclusions about intelligence. (When, in fact — as noted earlier — the test was originally designed to screen children who might be struggling with the curriculum, which is not necessarily the same thing as being intelligent or not [Lamiell, 2003].) Unfortunately, Stern was right in that

IQ tests would be misused and misapplied, sometimes tragically, as this chapter will show.

IQ tests were, and in many regards continue to be, premised on an archaic theory of intelligence called "general intelligence" or "G" intelligence. What we today recognise as spatial and logical-mathematical reasoning was seen as the basis of all human intelligence. The notion that a standardised test decrees a result that can be generalised as a marker of someone's achievement or ability is very much the active paradigm at work in high school end-of-year examinations or university entrance examinations. Instead of viewing these tests as *one* type of assessment looking at *one* dimension of intelligence among many others, they are taken to be all-encompassing measures of ability. This is a deeply fundamental flaw.

1.3   *Abuses*

Although the initial intention behind Binet's work was positive — in any case, it was looking to make the discourse on human intelligence more scientific, more granular, and less intuitive — the easier it became to administer the test, the more it was used in different contexts, which is where abusive use began.

In a chilling paper on the origins and early misuses of IQ tests, Reddy (2008) describes how IQ testing was used in the United States to classify people into groups of subintelligence: "Known as the father of intelligence testing in the United States, Goddard used a perversion of Binet's intelligence scale to rank those he considered feebleminded into varying degrees of mental incompetence: idiots (pre-verbal), imbeciles (illiterate), and morons (high functioning)" (p. 670).

In 1917, a variant of the IQ test was used to decide who would go to which grade in the army to fight in World War One. Since this variation was heavily biased toward "elite and urban pop culture" (Reddy, 2008, p. 672), immigrants and people of colour tended to score poorly and were therefore sent to the front lines. Anglo Saxon and Nordic test takers, on the other hand, who could relate to the test's references and style for cultural reasons, did better and found themselves in safer officer and administrative positions.

By 1927, the test was not only being used to identify so-called imbeciles but to sterilise them. The infamous *Buck v. Bell* case saw the U.S. Supreme Court uphold the sterilisation of Carrie Buck, who was diagnosed as "feeble minded", as were her parents (Reddy, 2008, p. 668). Part of the reason for this was that eugenics was very influential at the time; when working hand in glove with an easy-to-administer capability test, the results were catastrophic.

A parallel can be made with Nazi Germany, where the state used IQ scores to put to death children deemed as "subintelligent". According to Stephen Murdoch, author of *IQ: A Smart History of a Failed Idea*, "by the end of the war, the Nazis would kill well over two hundred thousand handicapped people, many of whom were diagnosed as feebleminded, which required the use of IQ tests to assess intellectual ability" (2007, p. 128).

2   Normal Distribution as a Fundamental Socioeconomic and Psychometric Principle

The broader world view behind IQ testing, which is very much the backdrop for the current assessment system that predominates in high schools, is normal distribution. This mathematical principle, propagated in the nineteenth century by thinkers like Gauss, organises measurements into a normal distribution curve.

The idea is that the majority of measurements (for example, test scores) will form a "norm"; higher or lower scores will deviate from the norm. However, as there are fewer deviations from the norm, the shape of the graph depicting the overall numbers diminishes, creating a sloping bell curve with the mass in the middle (which will have a central value of zero) and the minority stretching out by standard deviations left or right of the centre.

This measurement technique can be used for a number of quantifiable human traits: height, for example. There are fewer tall people than "average height" people, even fewer very tall people, and exceptionally few extremely tall people; this last category will comprise outliers. The same applies to degrees of shortness, from slightly shorter than the norm, to much shorter than the norm, to so much shorter than the norm that we are looking at a population group of very few people. Here again, the population size diminishes left and right of the centre of the graph, creating the bell curve.

This is how IQ test scores are distributed; likewise, examination results, grade averages, and test scores. Some assessment systems use criterion rather than norm-referenced marking, meaning that standards are not measured within a cohort against a statistical norm but according to written ideals. In theory, this should mean that results would not necessarily fall into a normal distribution because students are not competing against one another but against a fixed standard. However, most criterion-referenced assessment systems still use a normal distribution curve to determine grade boundaries.

This system of describing human traits has become so entirely ingrained in theory and practice, across multiple fields, that it seems almost impossible to undo. It would take a massive step of bold philosophical deconstruction to reconsider, entirely, the phenomenon of human trait distribution in order to overhaul the normal distribution system and replace it with something else.

This current system is premised on elitist ideas that go back as least as far as Aristotle's theories of virtue (Bobnich, 2017). In essence, the idea is that not all human beings, or animals, or even plants for that matter, are endowed with the same level of ability, prowess, beauty, or intellect. Some are stronger and better than others in a type of grading system. By "virtue", Aristotle meant "excellence". This hierarchical manner of viewing the world permeated Aristotle's view of the world. To give an example, in speaking of happiness, Aristotle says (my italics):

> [H]appiness is activity in accordance with virtue, it is reasonable that it should be in accordance with the *highest virtue*; and this will be that of the *best thing* in us. Whether it be reason or something else that is this element which is thought to be our natural guide and to take thoughts of things *noble and divine*, whether it be itself also divine or only the most divine element in us, the activity of this in accordance with its proper virtue will be perfect happiness. (*Nicomachean Ethics,* Book X, 1177a, 11–18)

The insistence on absolutes ("highest", "best", "noble", "divine", "perfect") illustrates this idea. This was part of Plato's earlier thinking, too, in his notion of the philosopher king, whereby a people could only be led by someone who was gifted and more insightful, better endowed morally and intellectually than others. Plato believed in the theory of the forms, allegorised in his famous depiction of the prisoners in the cave in his *Republic*. For Plato, we only glimpse shadows and fragments of a faultless world. A sizable portion of Ancient Greek philosophy was built on this concept of a perfect, divine form to which we all aspire. An emblem of this is the *kouros*, the statue of the upstanding youth that expresses the exemplary dimensions of corporeal beauty according to Greek standards. In this model of physical perfection, the ethos of much Ancient Greek thinking can be found: a sublime, perfect, other-worldly form that can never be duplicated in reality but is continually sought after in the arts, intellectual matters, and athletics.

The danger of this idealistic view is that it leads to a thought system whereby that which is venerated and pursued is extremely rare if not impossible to attain: at the very extreme of the normal distribution. The idea that what is of quality must be rare and unusual explains why the concepts of "average" and "popular" tend to take on negative connotations: if you describe a performance as average, it is hardly a compliment; nor is it considered particularly positive if you liken what someone does or thinks to what "everybody" does. Hidden in these disparaging descriptions of the norm is the elitist craving for excellence that so drastically distorts the assessment system.

Not only is there the problem of denying the norm in favour of the exception, there's also the question of the criteria used to create a distribution curve. Clearly, human beings can be sorted by ability against a given trait, but those same humans who might outperform or underperform others on a single trait might exhibit a very different capability on another trait. Indeed, we know from empirical experience that this is very true. The athlete might not rank similarly as a community healer; the intellectual might not rank as a financer; the creatively minded person might not show the same high levels of perspicuity in more dry, analytical matters.

However, in Plato's and Aristotle's visions, a few traits are generalised across all beings (e.g., "virtue", "mind"). This overgeneralisation establishes a rigid and all-dominating hierarchy, leaving no place for the multiple talents and gifts that people have in other areas. This is the idea behind general intelligence, as well: we are looking at one type of intelligence and one type only.

2.1   *An Obsession with Declarative Knowledge and Academic Skills*

Another assessment-system shortcoming that prevails at the end of high school — and, therefore, to a large extent, during earlier school life too — is the overreliance on declarative knowledge. Since the Middle Ages, the dominant mode of knowledge development in schools has been based on a catechistic model whereby students are made to learn statements by heart and regurgitate them under test conditions. This was the way that passages from the Bible were learnt for centuries.

It is true that since the nineteenth century there has been a considerable departure from that model: a number of higher-order tasks such as essay and commentary writing, more elaborate and varied assessments such as experiments, field work, projects, and research have entered the fold. However, the dominant assessment method globally is multiple choice (Butler, 2018), used in large-scale assessment scenarios such as national examinations and university admission tests.

The advantage of tests based on facts is that students have identical cultural references since they have been learnt by heart, to the letter, and will not have been distorted in any way from one learner to the next. If one of the superordinate goals of education is cultural transmission, then rote learning is a sure way of consolidating that. Multiple-choice tests eliminate rater bias: there is no real scope for interpretation as the answers are entirely factual. The cost of such testing is much cheaper; and, quite often, machines can mark the test.

The disadvantage of this assessment method is mainly that it measures one type of competence only, which is knowledge retention and regurgitation. Such a testing method favours students who can learn declarative knowledge by heart and recall it under test conditions. It does not give a chance to more creative responses, to longer, more associative and qualitative trains of thought, let alone to less academic competences.

Indeed, whether it be through multiple test assessments or other types of evaluation, academic knowledge is favoured overwhelmingly in the traditional, dominant testing regime. Examinations tend to be centred on knowledge and understanding of scientific, historical, literary, and theoretical constructs in the social sciences.

These high-stakes assessments influence the style of teaching and learning that takes place leading up to them: the pressure on teachers and students is for students to perform well on the tests. Since the tests are largely based on assessing declarative knowledge and academic test–taking ability, teachers must teach those skills. Students who could be advancing their learning in other areas — such as sports, arts, social impact work (like community service), intrapersonal and interpersonal skills–based activities (meditation, reflection, coaching, followership, and leadership) — must put these aside in order to conform to the overwhelming, solitary emphasis on academic factual knowledge.

2.2 *The Need to Go Further*

In sum, the problem is not necessarily that academic knowledge is tested in schools, and perhaps not even that student scores are laid out in a normal distribution curve, separating low from average-to-high scores. The problem is that there is little real space for alternatives, complementary assessment types, and mechanisms to report on other kinds of capability and proficiency. Academic knowledge and test-taking ability have their roles in education and suggest transferable skills (memorisation, understanding, reformulation) — but these comprise an unduly narrow set of skills to use for examinations that are so high stakes in nature.

If we were able to free our minds of the bell curve and think about people as bringing different and varied talents to the world rather than placed on one continuum, the effects would be liberating and would create a more inclusive understanding of what it means to be educated and what it means to be human.

References

Aristotle. In J. Barnes (Ed.). (1984). *The complete works of Aristotle: The revised Oxford translation*. Princeton University Press.

Bobonich, C. (2017). Elitism in Plato and Aristotle. In C. Bobonich (Ed.), *The Cambridge companion to ancient ethics* (pp. 298–318). Cambridge University Press.

Bulmer, M. (1999). The development of Francis Galton's ideas on the mechanism of heredity. *Journal of the History of Biology, 32*(3), 263–292. https://doi.org/10.1023/a:1004608217247

Butler, A. C. (2018). Multiple-choice testing in education: Are the best practices for assessment also good for learning? *Journal of Applied Research in Memory and Cognition, 7*(3), 323–331. https://doi.org/10.1016/j.jarmac.2018.07.002

Lamiell, J. T. (2003). *Beyond individual and group differences.* Sage.

Murdoch, S. (2007). *IQ: A smart history of a failed idea.* John Wiley & Sons.

Nicolas, S., Gounden, Y., & Piolino, P. (2013). Victor and Catherine Henri on earliest recollections. *L'Année psychologique, 113*(3), 349–374. https://doi.org/10.3917/anpsy.133.0349

Nicolas, S., Coubart, A., & Lubart, T. (2014). The program of individual psychology (1895–1896) by Alfred Binet and Victor Henri. *L'Année Psychologique, 114*(1), 5–60. https://doi.org/10.4074/S0003503314001 02x

Reddy, A. (2008). The eugenic origins of IQ testing: Implications for post-Atkins litigation. *De Paul Law Review, 57*(5).

CHAPTER 3

Checkerboards and Straightjackets
The Organisation of the Timetable and Grading Systems

1   The Carnegie Unit

If you walk into any high school, the first thing you will notice is the way that the working day is organised. The overwhelming majority of schools have a quasi-identical structure driven by a timetable whereby learning is structured into periods. These periods are often in the region of 40 to 60 minutes each; many will be grouped as "doubles" of one-and-a-half hours or two hours. Often a bell will ring, and students will pack their bags and shuffle to the next class, and then the next, until the day is over. The next day will resemble much of the first, and so on. This system often propagates itself from high school right down to primary school. It is only among much younger learners that the day is structured in a more fluid, transdisciplinary, and flexible manner, allowing for projects, extended learning, even naps and outdoor learning.

Where does this ritual come from? Why is it that this model predominates?

Throughout the Middle Ages and the Enlightenment, courses of study were not standardised and, therefore, varied greatly in length and assessment method. The length of a course and the way it was assessed was decided by its teacher. In the nineteenth century, as universities started to develop across the world, particularly in the United Kingdom and in the United States, admissions teams expressed frustration at the disparity in contact time that different students had experienced in their schooling. Some might have spent over 200 hours learning a subject; others, under 100. How would admissions officers compare such situations and vouch that the student had had the right amount of learning to be eligible for entry into the university? From an assessment point of view, we can see this as a problem of reliability — inconsistent testing methods make testing unfair for students.

Harvard president Charles William Eliot responded by proposing units considered necessary for the correct amount of study to have taken place (for more on this, see Silva, 2015). For Eliot, students would have to study a subject for 120 hours to gain credit. This meant that throughout a school year of 40 weeks — i.e., 52 weeks minus roughly 12 weeks for holidays (depending on the system) — each week would contain 3 hours of courses. These 3 hours would be divided evenly across a week to make it easier for the student to establish a rhythm of working and not to concentrate each course into tight packages. The typical model would be four separate periods of 45 minutes each. Assuming roughly 36 working hours per week (after taking out time for lunch and breaks), this would allow for up to 12 subjects to be studied over a year, divided into a set number of periods during a week.

Of course, this model has variations, especially when students go into more depth in certain subjects, taking them as majors or at a higher level. In such circumstances, students might study fewer subjects over the course of a year (6 to 8 subjects, versus 12).

At the end of the 1900s, this credit system was endorsed by the American National Education Association. From then on, high schools would have to ensure that students followed courses for 120 hours to be awarded credit (Shedd, 2003). However, adoption was slow; it was only between 1906 and 1910, when the Carnegie Foundation made this unit of study (120 hours) a mandatory institutional condition for college professors to receive their retirement pensions, that adoption became widespread. This is why the 120 hours of study, split into periods, is called the Carnegie Unit (Carnegie Foundation, 2023).

2   Standardised Curriculum Design

The need to standardise curriculum sequencing was done in order to make the course of study at high schools more reliable in the eyes of universities. By ensuring that a unit of study complied with minimal time requirements, the relative chaos and extreme variability of learning experiences that had hitherto made admissions criteria tenuous and subjective became much more objective.

However, in standardising study units across the curriculum, the Carnegie Unit was not just making the exposure to learning across different systems and schools comparable — it was also defining, substantively, what the experience of learning meant. The pace of learning would no longer be dictated by the needs of the student or the decisions of the teacher but by the need to get through the curriculum in a certain amount of time. This would lead to the artificial prolongation of some units and, perhaps more damaging, the contraction of others. Teachers and students rushed through some units in order to fit everything into a week, for example, as designed according to administrative, rather than pedagogic, exigencies.

Learning is a complex process in which educators should use time judiciously to meet the needs of students. According to needs, pacing, and individual challenges, the time dedicated to learning should be as flexible as possible.

Some concepts are more complex than others (for example, threshold concepts such as gravity in physics, moles in chemistry, or literary analysis), and teachers need more time to help students solidify their understanding of these.

Gifted students typically process information more quickly than other students; whereas students who struggle to access the curriculum will need more time as information is scaffolded and repeated, chunked and reinforced. It is unhelpful to consider the process of learning, which by nature is differentiated and individualised, in terms of standardised chunks of time.

So the Carnegie Unit of study — and the manner in which it has been subdivided into equally distributed units of time in school schedules — creates an artificially consistent rhythm of curriculum coverage, which does not meet the saccadic and irregular nature of learning. Many of the problems that students experience in their learning are not addressed because the approach is based on unit coverage rather than remedial work. In an interview on the cognition of understanding, developmental psychologist Howard Gardner pointed this out:

> The greatest enemy of understanding is coverage. As long as you are determined to cover everything, you actually ensure that most kids are not going to understand. You've got to take enough time to get kids deeply involved in something so they can think about it in lots of different ways and apply it — not just at school but at home and on the street and so on. (Brandt, 1993)

For a more valid learning experience, one in which students can thrive according to their needs, educators would need to design units of study differently, allowing for more time to go deep into understanding and application.

A restructured timetable would imply a restructured assessment system, too, since there would be fewer items to score — and what would be assessed would be depth of understanding rather than coverage of knowledge.

3   Grading: Technical, Emotional, and Psychological Effects

Central to the post–nineteenth-century system of curriculum coverage and assessment is grading. The origins of this practice are debated: for some it began at Yale (Pierson, 1983); for others, at Cambridge (Postman, 1992). What is clear is that, by the end of the 1700s in some universities, professors were dividing attainment into symbols, percentages, numbers, or letters, so as to organise results into categories.

The tendency has been to subdivide results numerically into bands of roughly 15%, from *A* to *E*. The common practice in high schools is for all work, or at least the vast majority of work, to be described through such a grading system.

Grading is less an act of formative assessment (meaning, assessment that helps students learn by giving them qualitative feedback on what they can do to improve) and more one of summative assessment (meaning, an act of judgement at the end of a piece of work to communicate to the student what that piece of work is worth).

It is understandable to want to quantify assessment into a neat and clear system that allows evaluators and learners to situate their attainment in a straightforward fashion. However, reams of educational research point out just how damaging grades can be for learning (e.g., Black & Wiliam, 1998; Butler, 2011; Putwain, 2009).

Pulfrey, Buchs, and Butera (2011) "revealed that expectation of a grade for a task, compared with no grade, consistently induced greater adoption of performance-avoidance, but not performance-approach, goals" (p. 683). The work of Dylan Wiliam (2001; 2017) has shown how grades wash out feedback on learning, focussing students' minds on ego and status rather than on steps for improvement.

Grades are not only considered to be particularly inefficient for learning but have several negative backwash effects on wellbeing. Högberg et al. (2021), looking at the effects of the introduction of grading in Swedish schools, found "negative health consequences of accountability policies such as testing and grading" and that there are "stronger effects on girls compared to boys [...] in line with studies suggesting that girls are more sensitive to performance-based self-esteem" (p. 1). Crocker et al. (2003), in studying the effects of grading on university students in the United States, found that "bad grades led to greater drops in self-esteem [which] predicted increases in depressive symptoms for students initially more depressed" (p. 507). Wang (2016) found similar outcomes in researching the effects of grading on teenagers.

And yet the ritual of grading is extremely strong in schools, anchored as a cultural norm that seems almost impossible to displace. This is not to say that experiments to move away from grading are not abundant, for they are. In fact, as Kohn (2013) points out, research going back as far as the 1930s and 1940s (Crooks, 1933; Linder, 1940; De Zouche, 1945) pointed out the dangers and inefficacy of grading, but to little avail.

As of the writing of this book, experiments to assess students beyond and outside of grading are outnumbered massively by the global juggernaut of grading throughout the world's high schools. I very much hope that anyone picking up this book 100 years from now will read it in an age where grading is seen as an antiquated system no longer in force.

4   Placement Tests and Cut-offs

Since grading systems are used primarily with a summative purpose (as opposed to a formative purpose), their most common application is to rank students for selection eligibility.

We can see several examples of this practice in different national systems. For example, the 11+ Test is administered to Year 6 students in some parts of the United Kingdom to determine entry into grammar schools (which are reputed to be academically rigorous). Students may only take the test once; it is essentially structured as a psychometric evaluation. In Switzerland, for students to enter the academic pathway leading to high-school certification, they must either sit examinations or obtain certain grades at the end of their middle schooling. In the United States, most universities require students to obtain certain scores on standardised admissions tests in order to be considered for admission; and in the United Kingdom, universities will set "tariffs" for entry, meaning that, to be admitted, students must achieve a certain grade at the end of high school.

Selective schools will demand that students submit either a certain grade average, a certain performance on a placement test, or a certain IQ test score in order to be considered for admission.

Schools running special education programmes or streams for gifted and talented students will often require certain IQ test scores to determine who gets into the course and who does not.

The purpose of these selective entry mechanisms is to make sure that students with a certain intellectual and/or cognitive profile are admitted. In most cases, this means that there is less pressure on the schools to raise admitted students' achievement since students entering the system are already academically groomed, good test-takers, and high achievers. One might ask what the fundamental educative purpose of selective educational systems is: since the premise of education should be to improve learning, it would make more sense for schools to accept the lower-scoring students in order to provide what is known as "value added" to their learning.

One problem that these selective mechanisms cause is the notion of the cut-off grade. Seemingly arbitrary numbers are used to determine whether students progress to a selective institution (or section of the institution) or not. Highly selective North American universities never quote an exact SAT or ACT score or grade average required for them to consider a student. Instead, they speak in "ranges" (Glassman & Swanston, 2024) — stressing the importance of a holistic appreciation of an application file and how the process involves admissions deans discussing student files and considering several factors (recommendations, personal statement, grade averages, standardised admissions test scores). However, given the vast number of applications and the difficulty of having to choose one student among a large pool with very similar scores, often a few points or one tenth of a grade-point average on a subject will be used to decide who is accepted and who is not.

Other systems are less subtle and determine very sharp cut-off points for entry. For example, in the 1920s, Terman (1926) claimed that students with an IQ of 140 or higher were "gifted". (For a more detailed analysis of IQ cut-off points to determine giftedness, see Mcbee & Makel, 2019.)

Card and Giuliano (2015) show how, in 2005, an unnamed US school district — described as "one of the largest and most diverse school districts in the country" (p. 1) — introduced a scheme whereby "non-disadvantaged students scoring above 130 points on [a type of IQ] test, and [second-language learners and students receiving free or reduced lunches] scoring above 115 points were eligible for referral for IQ testing" (p. 5). Such scores would, depending on subsequent IQ scores, lead to access to a remedial programme. The paper reveals how "relatively high ability students from disadvantaged backgrounds were being overlooked under the traditional referral system" (p. 3) and the "traditional referral system also misses some high ability non-disadvantaged students" (p. 15).

So the consequences of performing above or below a threshold — which can mean, for example, how students answer one question worth just a few points — can be significant and have all sorts of implications for students' future pathways, subsidies, or opportunities. Cut-offs are too narrow as criteria for major decisions on student opportunities; they result in many gifts being missed in the process. More enlightened assessment systems, such as those we explore later in this book, broaden assessment to prevent these narrow cut-off exercises. Unfortunately, they remain the exception: almost all British universities, for example, will select students based on a UCAS tariff points system with very sharp cut-offs.

5   Why Breaking the Checkerboard Is So Difficult

This assessment grid, from the Carnegie Unit to grading to cut-offs, is a tightly regulated and numerical checkerboard. Human potential, which is subtle, variable, culturally specific, and infinitely creative, sits uneasily on this checkerboard, never quite corresponding to its hard contours and angular delineations.

From Binet's work on IQ testing through two centuries of statistical modelling being the dominant paradigm in the behavioural sciences, this checkerboard has become hardened in the central role it plays in education. Entire districts, national education systems, and even global testing schemes rely on it as an axiomatic playing field that determines practices and decisions.

To break up this checkerboard and create something else will require major upheaval, a coordinated effort across several simultaneous matrices. The work will be difficult, but it is not impossible and must remain a hope, so that the way human beings are viewed and evaluated changes.

References

Black, P., & Wiliam, D. (1998). Assessment and classroom learning. *Assessment in Education: Principles, Policy & Practice, 5*(1), 7–74. https://doi.org/10.1080/0969595980050102

Brandt, R. (1993). *On teaching for understanding: A conversation with Howard Gardner.* ASCD. https://ascd.org/el/articles/on-teaching-for-understanding-a-conversation-with-howard-gardner

Butler, R. (2011). Enhancing and undermining intrinsic motivation: The effects of task-involving and ego-involving evaluation on interest and performance. *British Journal of Educational Psychology, 58*(1), 1–14. https://doi.org/10.1111/j.2044-8279.1988.tb00874.x

Card, D., & Giuliano, L. (2015). *Can universal screening increase the representation of low income and minority students in gifted education?* Working paper 21519. National Bureau of Economic Research.

Carnegie Foundation. (2023). *What is the Carnegie Unit?* https://www.carnegiefoundation.org/faqs/-carnegie-unit/

Crocker, J., Karpinski, A., Quinn, D. M., & Chase, S. K. (2003). When grades determine self-worth: Consequences of contingent self-worth for male and female engineering and psychology majors. *Journal of Personal and Social Psychology, 85*(3), 507–516. https://doi.org/10.1037/0022-3514.85.3.507. PMID: 14498786

Crooks, A. D. (1933). Marks and marking systems: A digest. *Journal of Educational Research, 27*(4), 259–272.

De Zouche, D. (1945). "The wound is mortal": Marks, honors, unsound activities. *The Clearing House, 19*(6), 339–344.

Glassman, S., & Swanston, B. (2024). Get accepted: What is the average SAT score needed for college admission? *Forbes Advisor* (updated February 7). https://www.forbes.com/advisor/education/student-resources/average-sat-score/

Högberg, B., Lindgren, J., Johansson, K., Strandh, M., & Petersen, S. (2021). Consequences of school grading systems on adolescent health: Evidence from a Swedish school reform. *Journal of Education Policy, 36*(1), 84–106. https://doi.org/10.1080/02680939.2019.1686540

Kohn, A. (2013). The case against grades. *Counterpoints, 451,* 143–153. http://www.jstor.org/stable/42982088

Mcbee, M., & Makel, M. (2019). The quantitative implications of definitions of giftedness. *AERA Open, 5*(1). https://doi.org/10.1177/2332858419831007

Meyer, J. H. F., & Land, R. (2006). Threshold concepts and troublesome knowledge: Issues of liminality. In J. H. F. Meyer & R. Land (Eds.), *Overcoming barriers to student understanding: Threshold concepts and troublesome knowledge* (pp. 19–32). Routledge.

Pierson, G. (1983). C. Undergraduate studies: Yale College. *A Yale book of numbers: Historical statistics of the college and university 1701–1976.* Yale Office of Institutional Research.

Postman, N. (1992). *Technopoly: The surrender of culture to technology.* Alfred A. Knopf.

Pulfrey, C., Buchs, C., & Butera, F. (2011). Why grades engender performance-avoidance goals: The mediating role of autonomous motivation. *Journal of Educational Psychology, 103*(3), 683–700. https://doi.org/10.1037/a0023911

Putwain, D. W. (2009). Assessment and examination stress in Key Stage 4. *British Educational Research Journal, 35*(3), 391–411. http://doi.org/10.1080/01411920802044404

Shedd, J. (2003). The history of the student credit hour. *New Directions for Higher Education, 122*(Summer), 5–12. http://doi.org/10.1002/he.106

Silva, E. (2015). *The Carnegie unit: A century-old standard in a changing education landscape.* Carnegie Foundation for the Advancement of Teaching.

Terman, L. M. (Ed.). (1926). *Genetic studies of genius: Mental and physical traits of a thousand gifted children* (Vol. 1, 2nd ed.). Stanford University Press.

Wang, L. C. (2016). The effect of high-stakes testing on suicidal ideation of teenagers with reference-dependent preferences. *Journal of Population Economics, 29*(2), 345–364. http://doi.org/10.1007/s00148-015-0575-7

Wiliam, D. (2001). What is wrong with our educational assessments and what can be done about it? *Education Review, 15,* 57–62.

Wiliam, D. (2017). *Embedded formative assessment.* 2nd ed. Solution Tree Press.

CHAPTER 4

The One-Size-Fits-All World of Mass Testing

1 The Origins, Purposes, and Development of Large-Scale Learning Assessments

Knowing how well students were doing across national systems was something that was only addressed after World War Two, when an interest in intergovernmental cooperation and worldwide rights to education arose with the creation of the United Nations. Hence, since the 1950s, large-scale learning assessments (LSLAs) have grown in application across the world education setting (Khorramdel et al., 2023). Large numbers of students are tested, usually at the same time, in order to derive attainment data that is used for accountability measures, target setting, and general analysis (Thurlow, 2010). The most popular and best known LSLAs are the TIMSS (Trends in International Mathematics and Science Study), PIRLS (Progress in International Reading Literacy Study), and PISA tests (Programme for International Student Assessment).

PISA scores have been used, to much public acclaim, to compare national systems: annual PISA results usually motivate the press and those interested in educational standards to rush to see which country has scored the highest in mathematics or literacy. Recent crazes for the pedagogic and assessment methods used in Finland, Japan, Singapore, and Switzerland have come from PISA results.

The intention behind these LSLAs has been to compare districts and national systems with regard to the efficacy of their educational interventions. Without these studies, it would be difficult to speak, globally, of literacy and numeracy scores — essential data for study and subsequent policy amendments by ministries of education and international organisations such as UNESCO, the OECD, and the World Bank. LSLAs allow organisations and governments to arrive at fundamentally important conclusions about education. A UNESCO (2019) paper on LSLAs states:

> LSLAs have never been as much in demand. They are now regarded as being critical to improve the quality of education and they have contributed greatly to strengthening policies and strategies aimed at enhancing effective and relevant learning. Increasingly used to ensure excellence in education, they are at the centre of discussions related to the quality and effectiveness of education systems at national, regional and global levels.

However, the paper also argues that "under certain circumstances, they may unintentionally undermine the Education 2030 commitments made to ensure relevant, equitable and quality learning for all". This is because "LSLAs are by design generally limited to a small number of easily-measurable areas of learning that lend themselves to system-level or cross-country comparability" (p. 34). Furthermore, "children with moderate to severe permanent physical disabilities, those with cognitive, behavioral or emotional disabilities as well as those with insufficient language experience tend to be excluded [from LSLAs]" (pp. 45–46).

Indeed, a backwash effect of LSLA testing, especially with the pressure that might come from different constituencies reading through the results as an indication of accountability, is that the test takes over the learning process. That is, systems and districts become more concerned with PISA results than the less immediately quantifiable and more subtle business of student learning. This is a typical danger of high-stakes assessments, which tend to interrupt the mindful and epistemically localised pace of learning required to consolidate deep understanding in the classroom.

In 2014, a large group of educational authorities, mainly academics, signed a scathing open letter in *The Guardian*, directed at the OECD. It states:

> [The] OECD's narrow focus on standardised testing risks turning learning into drudgery and killing the joy of learning. As Pisa has led many governments into an international competition for higher test scores, OECD has assumed the power to shape education policy around the world, with no debate about the necessity or limitations of OECD's goals. We are deeply concerned that measuring a great diversity of educational traditions and cultures using a single, narrow, biased yardstick could, in the end, do irreparable harm to our schools and our students. (Andrews et al., 2014)

In a similar vein, and in relation to standardised testing in general, in a powerful paper published in 1988, the National Association for the Education of Young Children (NAEYC) states, pertinently:

> Ironically, the calls for excellence in education that have produced widespread reliance on standardized testing may have had the opposite effect — mediocrity. Children are being taught to provide the one "right" answer on the answer sheet, but are not being challenged to think. Rather than producing excellence, the overuse (and misuse) of standardized testing has led to the adoption of appropriate teaching practices as well as admission and retention policies that are not in the best interests of individual children or the nation as a whole.

Notwithstanding technical assessment problems with generalising the results of LSLAs,[1] there are benefits to them — notably, the type of metrics that can be drawn up to make global and national conclusions about learning. However, they pose a number of problems that are common to mass testing.

2   Assessment Problems Created by Mass Testing

The challenges created by LSLAs are generic to the world of mass testing, which is a major obstacle to deep learning and to the recognition of true human gifts. Indeed, the massive scale itself of examinations forces their developers to pare down what they are testing into heavily reduced and ultimately invalid constructs. At the least, they are invalid in so far as the competences necessary for the workplace and human flourishing are more subtle, expansive, and intertwined than what can be tested through multiple-choice or item-response examinations.

Large curriculum boards began to operate after World War Two alongside the proliferation of United Nations organisations, nationwide curriculum reforms, and efforts to provide education to vast numbers of people. Examinations like the O-levels (reformed to GCSEs — General Certificate in Secondary Education — in the 1980s) and A-levels in England, and Advanced Placement in the United States came into force in the early 1950s.

Other large-scale examination boards were older; for example, the Baccalauréat in France was instituted at the beginning of the nineteenth century by Napoleon Bonaparte. Whether they were invented centuries ago or more recently, they have all undergone successive reforms, essentially to make them more centralised.

The philosophical driver for examination boards is a macroscopic approach that considers learning as something that should happen across an entire nation so as to create generations of people who share the same or similar codes, cultural epistemes, and skills. Wide-scale educational reform influences nation-state identity. Furthermore, since post–World War Two studies in economics show, convincingly, the positive correlation between education and economic growth (Lewis, 1962), governments have focussed on nationwide educational reform as one of their priorities.

Literacy rates are increasing because of this: in the early 1900s they were at roughly 20%; today, estimates are 87% (Buchholz, 2022). This is clearly a good thing. However, this emphasis on literacy and numeracy obscures the development of other skills that might be important in a country's culture — but are not measured. For example, which languages are being measured in the global

statistics on literacy levels? As this book progresses and we explore the competences necessary for a broader appreciation of the human condition and the
world of work, we will see how very few of those competences are assessed. A
culture of mass testing means that a narrow panel of skills is brought to the
fore, at the expense of many others.

3   **The Cultural Hegemony of Assessment Centralisation and How
       This Affects Learners in Different Parts of the World**

One of the major problems created by large-scale assessments is that of curriculum relevance. For learning to be meaningful, it should be contextual-
ised: what is learnt in school will be deployed mainly in a national, culturally
specific context unless students are studying an international curriculum. Of
course, there is an argument that we live in a globalised economy and that
what we learn in school should be set in a global context. This line of thinking
would support the uniformisation of curriculum and assessment — as well as
the language of instruction — so as to prepare students to be able to function
anywhere in the world, no matter where they were studying.

    However, this is not the reality in many schools following a highly central-
ised curriculum experience, especially in many parts of the so-called Global
South. Much of this is to do with the legacy of colonialism, which used a standardised curriculum as a vehicle to constrict thinking into a uniform worldview
(Manse, 2022). Philosophers such as Sen (2009) and Ngugi wa Thiong'o (1986)
have explained how educational reform can uproot students from their own
cultures, subjecting them to a type of supra-cultural framework that is not
immediately relevant to their needs or aspirations and, in fact, is there to keep
them in place socially — in many ways creating limitations more than eman-
cipation. This was the explicit intention of British colonisation in India, for
example, as exemplified in the nineteenth-century Macaulay Papers. These
documents make it quite clear that the purpose of the curriculum in British
colonial India was to uproot Indians from their local culture and limit the horizon of their thinking within the parameters of colonial control.

    Since decolonisation in the middle to end of the twentieth century across
Africa and Asia, the reappropriation of local culture in the curriculum has only
been partial. Numerous critics (see, for instance, Moncrieffe, 2020; Mukherjee,
2018; Ndille, 2020) point out that the project to create national curricula across
independent countries turned into a neocolonial exercise whereby most
textbooks and curricula material were transported from another culture and
language.

A study of primary-school textbooks in Tanzania (Haulle & Kabelege, 2021) found "that there are too few supplementary books in Kiswahili language as compared to those in the English language" (p. 12). They also found that "learners and teachers who use English as the medium of instruction have plenty of choice as many authors write their books in that language. Such books are also imported from other countries" (p. 13). The article includes extracts from the textbooks reminding children to stay out of the sun and use parasols, which seem like curious messages to be sending to schoolchildren in Africa. As a consequence, "choices for learners and teachers who are using Kiswahili language as a medium of instruction are extremely limited, which helps to perpetuate the existing class divide within the Tanzanian society" (p. 28).

Bose and Gao (2022) found an overrepresentation of white, British, and male characters in English textbooks in India. Akkari and Radhouane (2022) explain how representations of diversity in Brazilian textbooks are recent — about 20 years old — against a context of European culturally hegemonic representation.

To continue with the Brazilian example, the Bolsonaro government declared that it would review textbooks because there was a left-leaning agenda, influenced by Paolo Freire's radical school of thought, that needed to be purged (Cardin, 2020). Similarly, authorities in the state of Florida went about purging textbooks of material they considered ideological because of their references to historical facts, such as slavery, or their showing images of Rosa Parks, a civil rights leader (Tolin, 2023).

The point here is that centralised curricula become the battleground of political agendas. In the current century, efforts at the level of curriculum composition have undone some of the underrepresentation, overrepresentation, or biased representation of certain groups marked by the colonial and neocolonial era of textbook production. However, conservative voices are contesting these reforms and reverting some of those curricula to less diverse representations of social, historical figures in the making of the nation-state. This creates a pendulum effect and puts into question the real relevance of the curriculum for learners, since it is used as an instrument to shape minds rather than a reflection of a generation's needs and interests. Indeed, the Florida and Brazil examples have caused much consternation from scholars and students who, on the whole, are in favour of more equitable representation of diverse groups in the curriculum.

The flooding of the educational world by Large Language Models (LLMs) — which scrape the internet for the most statistically predominant images, phrases, and general semantic configurations — has exacerbated this challenge of designing representational curricula. LLMs have created heavily biased representations of professions and other social constructs (Ray, 2023). As students increasingly use these representations, whether such are structured in a curriculum or not, the importance of mitigating their effects through schooling becomes more salient. Students need to discuss and problematise information generated on the web, which is not something that a massified standardised curriculum will achieve very easily. This leads us back to the problem of wooden truths and oversimplified realities being painted by assessment and curriculum schemes (or algorithms) built for a wide audience and not for more culturally specific groups.

4   The Language of Testing: Pitfalls and Inequities

One of the fundamental pitfalls of large-scale testing, whether it be in the form of LSALs or national curriculum board assessments, is the language used and the manner in which it is used — in terms of both the type of technical assessment-driven language and the cultural expression — which is not at all ergonomic or easily accessible to all types of learner. These create a problem of assessment validity known as "ecological validity", meaning that test takers are put at a disadvantage not because of the test's intrinsic content but because of the style in which it is presented to them. Often, it is minority groups that bear the brunt of this disadvantage.

As far back as the 1980s, some were criticising the manner in which standardised tests were narrowing the construct of understanding into excessively technical dimensions of knowledge:

> [A] whole language/literacy approach that integrates oral language, writing, reading, and spelling in a meaningful context, emphasiz[es] comprehension. However, standardized tests of reading achievement still define reading exclusively as phonics and word recognition and measure isolated skill acquisition. Similarly, current theory of mathematics instruction stresses the child's construction of number concepts through first-hand experiences, while achievement tests continue to define mathematics as knowledge of numerals. (Meier, 2024)

Meier (2024), in looking at assessments from the 1980s explains how "a third of the items in typical reading achievement tests [were] dialect prejudiced. For example, they require[d] minority students to make distinctions between words, removed from context, which [were] often homonyms". This is still the case to a large extent in language assessments (Elder, 2012).

Literacy rates in and coming out of many sub-Saharan African schools are, globally speaking, low.[2] Why is this? A core reason is language:

> It has always been felt by African educationists that the African child's major learning problem is linguistic. Instruction is given in a language that is not normally used in his immediate environment, a language which neither the learner nor the teacher understands and uses well enough. (Obanya, 1980, p. 88)

The language of instruction in many African countries is French, Portuguese, or English. This creates "difficulties that arise when teachers neither speak nor understand the languages of the children they teach, especially in remote areas [...], contributing to low performance of children in school" (Van Pinxteren, 2022).

Reforming the language of instruction, a longstanding objective for curriculum relevance, means radically reconceptualising learning environments. It means localising learning and effectively doing away with the broad, arguably neocolonial globalised brushstrokes of a monolithic, homogenous linguistic and cultural approach — to create something that is heterogenous, multiple, and flexible.

Reforming assessment will be key in getting closer to this objective. What needs to be changed is not only content but assessment and, more radical still, language.

Notes

1 Scherer, Siddiq, & Nilsen (2024) show how it is problematic using LSLAs in meta-analyses to draw conclusions about the effectiveness of educational interventions at a clustered, global scale.

2 More than 30% of Malian youths aged 15–19 years who completed 6 years of schooling could not read a simple sentence; the same was true of more than 50% of Kenyan youths (World Bank, 2011).

References

Akkari, A., & Radhouane, M. (2022). Intercultural education in Brazil. In A. Akkari & M. Radhouane (Eds.), *Intercultural approaches to education* (pp. 95–104). Springer. https://doi.org/10.1007/978-3-030-70825-2_7

Andrews, A., Atkinson, L., Ball, S. J., Barber, M., Beckett, L., Berardi, J., ... & Zhao, Y. (2014, May 6). OECD and Pisa tests are damaging education worldwide — Academics.

Open letter to Dr Andreas Schleicher, director of the OECD's Programme for International Student Assessment. *The Guardian.* https://www.theguardian.com/education/2014/may/06/oecd-pisa-tests-damaging-education-academics

Bose, P., & Gao, X. (2022). Cultural representations in Indian English language teaching textbooks. *SAGE Open, 12*(1), 215824402210821. https://doi.org/10.1177/21582440221082102

Buchholz, K. (2022, September 12). This is how much the global literacy rate grew over 200 years. *World Economic Forum.* https://www.weforum.org/stories/2022/09/reading-writing-global-literacy-rate-changed/

Cardin, A. (2020). Bolsonaro calls today's Brazilian textbooks "garbage". *Rio Times.* https://www.riotimesonline.com/brazil-news/brazil/bolsonaro-calls-todays-textbooks-in-brazil-garbage/

Elder, C. (2012). Bias in language assessment. In C. Chapel (Ed.), *Encyclopaedia of applied linguistics.* Wiley-Blackwell. https://doi.org/10.1002/9781405198431.wbeal1198

Haulle, E., & Kabelege, E. (2021). Relevance and quality of textbooks used in primary education in Tanzania: A case of social studies textbooks. *Contemporary Education Dialogue, 18*(1), 12–28. https://doi.org/10.1177/0973184920962702

Khorramdel, L., von Davier, M., Kirsch, I., & Yamamoto, K. (2023). Educational surveys: Conceptual overview. In R. J. Tierney, F. Rizvi, & K. Ercikan (Eds.), *International encyclopedia of education* (4th ed., pp. 347–358). Elsevier.

Lewis, W. A. (1962). Education and economic development. *International Social Science Journal, 14*(4), 685–699.

Manse, M. (2022). Performing power: Cultural hegemony, identity, and resistance in colonial Indonesia, by Arnout van der Meer [Book review]. *Journal of the Humanities and Social Sciences of Southeast Asia, 178*(2–3), 345–348. https://doi.org/10.1163/22134379-17802007

Meier, T. (2024). The case against standardized achievement tests. *Rethinking Schools, 3*(2). https://rethinkingschools.org/articles/the-case-against-standardized-achievement-tests/

Moncrieffe, M. (2020). *Decolonising the history curriculum: Euro-centrism and primary schooling.* Palgrave Macmillan.

Mukherjee, M. (2018). Decolonizing pedagogy for inclusive education: Tagorean analysis of a case study. In K. J. Kennedy & J. J. Chi-kin Le (Eds.), *Routledge international handbook of schools and schooling in Asia* (pp. 709–721). Routledge.

Ndille, R. (2020). Schools with invisible fences in the British Southern Cameroons, 1916–1961: Colonial curriculum and the "other" side of modernist thinking. *Third World Quarterly, 42*(5), 1033–1051. http://dx.doi.org/10.1080/01436597.2020.1744431

NAEYC [National Association for the Education of Young Children]. (1988). *Young children, 43*(3).

Obanya, P. (1980). Research on alternative teaching in Africa. In E. A. Yoloye & J. Flechsig (Eds.), *Educational research for development* (pp. 67–112). Deutsche Stiftung für Internationale Entwicklung.

Ray, P. P. (2023). ChatGPT: A comprehensive review on background, applications, key challenges, bias, ethics, limitations and future scope. *Internet of Things and Cyber-Physical Systems, 3,* 121–154. https://doi.org/10.1016/j.iotcps.2023.04.003

Scherer, R., Siddiq, F., & Nilsen, T. (2024). The potential of international large-scale assessments for meta-analyses in education. *Large-scale Assessments in Education, 12*(4). https://doi.org/10.1186/s40536-024-00191-1

Sen, A. (2009). *The idea of justice.* Belknap Press of Harvard University Press.

Thurlow, M. L. (2010). Large-scale assessment and accountability and students with special needs. In P. Peterson, E. Baker, & B. McGaw (Eds.), *International encyclopedia of education* (3rd ed., pp. 752–758). Elsevier.

Tolin, L. (2023, March 16). Revised Florida textbooks left race out of Rosa Parks history. *Pen America.* https://pen.org/florida-textbooks-rosa-parks-history/

UNESCO. (2019). *The promise of large-scale learning assessments: Acknowledging limits to unlock opportunities.* https://unesdoc.unesco.org/ark:/48223/pf0000369697/PDF/369697eng.pdf.multi

van Pinxteren, B. (2022). Language of instruction in education in Africa: How new questions help generate new answers. *International Journal of Educational Development, 88.* https://doi.org/10.1016/j.ijedudev.2021.102524

wa Thiong'o, N. (1986). *Decolonizing the mind: The politics of language in African literature.* James Currey.

World Bank. (2011). *Education strategy 2020: Learning for all—Investing in people's knowledge and skills to promote development.* https://documents1.worldbank.org/curated/en/685531468337836407/pdf/644870WP0Learn00Box0361538B0PUBLIC0.pdf

CHAPTER 5

Covid-19 and the General Collapse of Traditional Assessment Systems

Covid-19 caused several systems and processes associated with the world of education and work to collapse: people were isolated, transmission models had to go online, classes were separated if not disbanded altogether. The consequences of Covid-19 were devastating for schools. The pandemic affected, adversely, "nearly 1.6 billion learners in more than 190 countries and all continents. Closures of schools and other learning spaces [...] impacted 94 per cent of the world's student population, up to 99 per cent in low and lower-middle income countries" (UN, 2020). In fact, the pandemic was the single largest disruptor to the education system seen worldwide in the last 50 years.

Much has been written about the severity of this upheaval and the implications for learning (Lewin, 2020; Hughes, 2020). Research has shown that mathematics and reading achievements dropped significantly because of Covid-19, primarily in 2020 and 2021 (Kuhfeld et al., 2022). Furthermore, the social disruption and sense of alienation caused by the pandemic and by institutional responses to the pandemic were palpable, leading to what some have called the creation of a "lost generation" (UNICEF, 2022). The resultant learning gaps were more or less potent according to the economic situation of the affected countries. "The World Bank estimates that while students in high-income countries gained an average of 50 harmonized learning outcomes (HLO) points a year pre-pandemic, students in low-income countries were gaining just 20, leaving those students several years behind" (Bryant et al., 2022).

Indeed, the problems of socioeconomic inequality that large-scale assessment models are trying to solve by widening access and making assessment relatively cheap were exacerbated when these models fell apart.

What Covid-19 showed the world of education was how much that world depended on examinations — and how fragile it was if and when this evaluation system was damaged or removed.

1 An Analysis of the Inability of Examination Boards to Survive 2020

The most significant effect of Covid-19 on assessment was the implosion of external examinations. A-levels, the French Baccalaureate, International

Baccalaureate, and numerous other examination boards were cancelled because of safety regulations concerning the pandemic, making it essentially impossible to hold live examinations. This sent school systems into a panic as they tried to find alternative ways of assessing students so as to formulate some sort of summative grade.

It was an opportunity to think creatively and wisely about how to assess students without end-of-year examinations. In my school (The International School of Geneva), for students in the lower years of high school — which run without an external examination board — we designed projects that learners could complete at home, giving them a chance to express themselves fully through an open-ended task. We also held oral *viva voces* online so as to allow a conversation between the teacher and the student on learning. The emotions of learning influenced some of the thinking behind these alternative assessments since anxiety was high among students, and assessment design needed to take this into account. It was also an opportunity to think more broadly about what we were assessing and why.

However, in large-scale assessment systems, such as examination boards and national curricula schemes, alternatives were derived in a very different manner. These were mainly made up of calculations based on historical trends in school- and student-performance data. In the UK, teachers were told to "submit the grade they thought their students would have likely achieved if they had taken their exams [and] to rank their students within cohorts of those they judged likely to get the same grade, from most to least likely" (Timsit, 2020). The grades generated through this process were then standardised by a regulatory body using an algorithm that factored into its calculations the past performances of students and the school. The results were fairly disastrous: roughly "40% of A-level grades were downgraded from teachers' assessments, meaning that students received lower grades than the ones expected by universities as a condition of enrollment" (Timsit, 2020). Students from lower-income families were downgraded even more.

The International Baccalaureate went through a similar process to that in the UK (Fitzgerald, 2023), calculating student scores based on coursework, teacher predictions, and the school's history of predicting grades accurately (or not). This led to a flattening of the assessment bell curve and, consequently, a number of potential top scorers to underperform. This caused much anger among stakeholders and led to the press' deeming the exercise a "scandal".

In France, students were awarded with grades that were "an average of their grades throughout the year, minus any grades obtained during the lockdown" (Fitzgerald, 2023). As a result, the pass rate was close to 96% — a considerable inflation of previous pass rates — and 10,000 new university places had to be created to accommodate the surplus of undergraduate students.

None of these alternatives was satisfactory, and all were clearly the results of an entire infrastructure built on the foundations of summative assessment. Once these high-stakes, narrow gates were broken, alternative paths had to be carved precipitously, not in order to ensure student learning but to generate results at all costs. Because of this, the assessment cornerstone of fairness was damaged.

In trying to solve the problem of generating grades for students without the primary mechanism used to create those grades (examinations), instead of divergent thinking, which might have taken assessment down a very different path, the approach was one of convergent thinking: looking for as close a proxy to examinations as possible and essentially attempting to do things the same way they had been done before.

Some systems, like the Advanced Placement (AP) in the United States, were able to shift online and retain the examination format without the face-to-face structure. This provided some continuity in the assessment system. However, those countries that did not examine students online used quantitative methods to describe outcomes, continuing to view student scores in a mean distribution curve. In fact, it was the science of grade creation rather than the core experience of learning that took over the process. This is not surprising given the sorting function of summative assessment, which — as I've said earlier in this book — is less about creating learning and more about judging performance. What the pandemic experience did was to exacerbate this reality.

2 The Return to "Normal": No Lessons Learned

During the Covid-19 pandemic, when schools and many offices were closed, students and teachers were online, and the whole structure of the working week had been disrupted, there was a promise in the air of this being a learning opportunity — that coming out of the process schools and universities would be able to take whatever learnings had been gathered to create a "new tomorrow". However, that never really happened.

Zhao and Watterston (2021) identified the following major changes that Covid-19 had the potential to bring about: "curriculum that is developmental, personalized, and evolving; pedagogy that is student-centered, inquiry-based, authentic, and purposeful; and delivery of instruction that capitalizes on the strengths of both synchronous and asynchronous learning" (p. 3). The first two points became clear to educators during the pandemic precisely because the massive structure of standardised testing could not be sustained; it became clear that in order to continue learning, the whole assessment approach would need to be broken down into more localised and flexible units.

The International Commission on the Futures of Education (UNESCO, 2020) stated that, after Covid-19, "we cannot return to the world as it was before". It noted that, among the changes needed to bring about a better educational system post-pandemic, was a review of the institutionalised and standardised model of schooling so as to explore more intentionally "individual study, group work, one-on-one meetings with teachers, research projects, citizen science, community service, and performance" (2020).

For Fernando Reimers (2021), the post-pandemic imperative was, "at the school or system level, [to] revisit the competencies that students are expected to have gained by the end of each grade, and focus on supporting the development of those competencies (rather than simply 'covering the curriculum')" (p. 18).

The idea of a competence-based curriculum framework is not new, but the experience of the pandemic strongly reinforced the need to adjust systems and processes to this effect, taking into account questions of wellbeing, personal agency, creativity, and learning to live together in an increasingly complex, interconnected world. The danger of future pandemics disrupting large-scale assessment design also meant that, by necessity, educators had to explore some alternative methods, including those that would support learners in low-infrastructure settings where access to a broadband connection is scarce and the option of moving examinations online is not viable.

However, despite the identified opportunities and the clear desire from many quarters to change systems for a more life-worthy and future-proof assessment system, the vast majority of schools reverted to the pre-2019 model following the lifting of Covid-19 restrictions.

To give an example, during the Covid years, the International Baccalaureate Diploma Programme restructured the assessment model by removing some of the examination papers and internal assessment exigencies: students graduated with a lighter assessment model (one examination rather than two in literature; two papers instead of three for the sciences, etc.). This was addressing the problem of curriculum load that affects so many high-school students — whereby the sheer volume of the curriculum makes it very difficult for students to muster deep understanding across such a broad range of tasks, as well as negatively affecting them psychologically and emotionally.

However, come 2023, the International Baccalaureate brought back the full battery of tests that make up the extremely rigorous 2019 assessment model of the Diploma. Instead of seizing the opportunity presented by the realities of Covid-19 to rethink the assessment model, lighten it quantitatively to create

more depth qualitatively, and at the same time respond to questions of ecological validity, the Baccalaureate chose a "back to normal" routine.

In the UK, "the sharp drop in grades in A-level results in England [in 2023]
ha[d] little to do with this particular cohort's ability. It [was], instead, the result
of a government strategy to get A-level results back to pre-pandemic levels, after
the soaring grade inflation of the Covid years" (Wheale, 2023). What this meant,
concretely, was that 2023 was a particularly difficult year for students, with
tougher grade boundaries and lower scores, as was the case before Covid-19.

It is worth reflecting on the fact that the students who had to face this
"return to normal" had also been affected by the pandemic, only earlier in
their learning. Thus, the logic of reverting to a pre-pandemic system was not
focused on the student experience but, rather, on the macro analysis of scores
across the entire system, which had to be normalised. This type of statistical
approach fails to take into account the individual student experience and is a
patent example of how the whole machinery of large-scale assessments fails
to do this.

If one walks through high schools today, the learning environment is very
similar to what it was before the pandemic: students tend to be sitting in rows
with a predominantly teacher-centred, didactic method. When this is not
the case (and it's important not to overgeneralise when making judgemental
comments about classroom pedagogy because there are remarkable, forward-
looking practitioners in the field), what one can be sure of is that the end of
the last two years of high school continue to be focused disproportionately on
grade attainment, examination papers, mark schemes — how to score points
rather than how to learn.

If one major change in teaching and learning has occurred due to the experience of the pandemic, it is the use of technology. Schools employ technology,
by and large, in more innovative and flexible ways than before the pandemic,
allowing for more blended and hybrid learning. The question is, has this
improved assessment and curriculum fundamentally, or just made the same
model more accessible? In fact, many students commented on how tiring
and monotonous online learning was during the lockdown, with a transmission model at the centre, limited interaction, and repetitive lesson schemes.

A number of universities followed a similar arc of reverting to pre-pandemic
practices shortly after the lockdown. Yale and Dartmouth decided to revert to
standardised tests instead of being "test optional" as they had been during and
just after the pandemic. Their argument was that data showed fewer disadvantaged students' being able to access university places through a test-optional
structure (Saul, 2024). This is something we will explore in greater detail in the
next chapter of this book.

3   The Future of High-Stakes Assessments in an Increasingly Unpredictable World

In a UNESCO report, Huong and Shwabe (2022) point out that "the benefits of high-stakes exams are widely recognized, as they are seen as an objective test for the validation of student learning and not affected by subjective assessment and stereotyping" (p. 14). Indeed, large-scale examinations do have some positive features, as their proponents point out. At the core of the philosophy behind this type of assessment are notions of fairness and objectivity. However, the UNESCO report also recognises that

> they [high-stakes exams] may not always be the solution for achieving equitable educational opportunities for all as they disadvantage students with difficulties to deal with pressure, poorer students who cannot afford private tutoring, labelling children as failures or focusing uniquely on the test curriculum rather than on individual learning needs. (Huong & Shwabe, 2022, p. 14)

So the problem of equity is not necessarily solved by large-scale solutions. This is a major factor to consider *especially* when the stakes are particularly high, for it is under these circumstances that the extra pressure on students and parents will drive them to look for material and pedagogic aids that poorer students cannot afford, actually widening the inequality gap. Moreover, examinations tend to magnify the damaging effects of prioritising curriculum coverage over learning.

If educators or others do create alternative assessment systems, they need to take into account problems of reliability since alternative systems have a tendency to be much more subjective — thus potentially less fair. However, the response cannot be to remain anchored in the traditional assessment system, for this does not solve the problem, either. We must bring an entirely new and imaginative design to the forefront of high-school assessment if we want change to be substantive and meaningful.

The experience of Covid-19 shook the foundations of high-school assessment, right at its most sensitive pressure point: the end-of-school qualification. How ready are we for future disruptions of this magnitude? The answer is that we are not ready until a more resilient and sustainable assessment system is in place.

References

Bryant, J., Child, F., Espinosa, J., Dorn, E., Hall, S., Schmautzer, D., Kola-Oyeneyin, T., ... & Woord, B. (2022, April 4). *How Covid-19 caused a global learning crisis*. Mckinsey &

Company. https://www.mckinsey.com/industries/education/our-insights/how-covid-19-caused-a-global-learning-crisis#/

Fitzgerald, S. (2023). Covid-19 and the International Baccalaureate: A computer-assisted discourse analysis of the IB scandal. *British Journal of Educational Studies, 71*(2), 129–148. http://doi.org/10.1080/00071005.2022.2056575

Hughes, C. (2020). Covid-19 and the opportunity to design a more mindful approach to learning. *Prospects, 49,* 69–72. https://doi.org/10.1007/s11125-020-09492-z

Huong, L. T., & Schwabe, M. (2022). *High-stakes exams and assessments during the Covid-19 crisis: What is the status at the end of the 2020–2021 school year?* Programme and meeting document. UNESCO. https://unesdoc.unesco.org/ark:/48223/pf0000381686

Kuhfeld, M., Soland, J., & Lewis, K. (2022). *Test score patterns across three Covid-19–impacted school years.* Annenberg Institute, Brown University. https://doi.org/10.26300/ga82-6v47

Lewin, K. M. (2020). Contingent reflections on coronavirus and priorities for educational planning and development. *Prospects, 49,* 17–24. https://doi.org/10.1007/s11125-020-09480-3

Reimers, F. (2021). *Education and Covid-19: Recovering from the shock created by the pandemic and building back better.* Educational Practices Series 34. UNESCO International Bureau of Education, & International Academy of Education. https://unesdoc.unesco.org/ark:/48223/pf0000378626

Saul, S. (2024, February 22). Yale to require standardized test scores for admissions. *New York Times.* https://www.nytimes.com/2024/02/22/us/yale-standardized-testing-sat-act.html

Timsit, A. (2020, August 19). France has a lesson for the UK in giving fair grades during a pandemic. *QUARTZ.* https://qz.com/1893452/frances-baccalaureate-handled-covid-19-better-than-uk-a-levels

UN [United Nations]. (2020, August). *Education during Covid-19 and beyond.* Policy brief. https://unsdg.un.org/resources/policy-brief-education-during-covid-19-and-beyond

UNESCO. (2020). *Education in a post-Covid world: Nine ideas for public action.* UNESCO International Commission on the Futures of Education. https://en.unesco.org/sites/default/files/education_in_a_post-covid_world-nine_ideas_for_public_action.pdf

UNICEF. (2022, November 18). *UNICEF calls for averting a lost generation as Covid-19 threatens to cause irreversible harm to children's education, nutrition and well-being.* Press release. https://www.unicef.org/press-releases/unicef-calls-averting-lost-generation-covid-19-threatens-cause-irreversible-harm

Wheale, S. (2023, August 17). A "glide path" to pre-Covid: Why A-level grades are lower in England this year. *The Guardian.* https://www.theguardian.com/education/2023/aug/17/a-glide-path-to-pre-covid-why-a-level-grades-are-lower-in-england-this-year

Zhao, Y., & Watterston, J. (2021). The changes we need: Education post Covid-19. *Journal of Educational Change, 22*(1), 3–12. http://doi.org/10.1007/s10833-021-09417-3. PMCID: PMC7890782

Politics and University Admissions

The Chokehold

Why exactly is the narrow, high-stakes summative assessment model so resolutely anchored, so firmly in place? If schools, examinations, and curriculum boards uphold this design, it is mainly because the end of high school is
a qualification that is a highly politicised entity and has become an expression of nation-state identity. In Baird, Isaacs, Opposs, and Grey's illuminating
Examination Standards: How Measures and Meanings Differ around the World
(2018), the full force of standard-setting bodies — how they collaborate and
the outcome of their work — is analysed in great detail. Discussions about
exactly what should be on the end-of-high-school examinations are by no
means straightforward and often lead to quarrels. After all, deciding what students should know in history, which texts they should have read in literature,
and which approach to the social sciences they should learn is as much a philosophical and even ideological discussion as it is a technical, pedagogic one.

The ultimate standards-setting arbitrator, therefore, tends to be the department, ministry, or secretary of education. Since democratic processes mean
that different governments with different approaches to education take control, standards and content can change, turning national curricula into a type
of playground of politics. Controversy over the teaching of slavery in Florida in
2023 is a case in point (Alvarez, 2023).

Whereas canons of knowledge were fairly homogenised throughout the
Middle Ages (Aristotle and Euclid in Europe, for example), as knowledge
has expanded and become more specialised — especially the case since the
Enlightenment — it has over time become very difficult to decide what every
young person should know and be able to do for an external judge to say that
they are "qualified" in some sense. With the rapid pace of change, increasingly
powerful artificial intelligence in the workplace, and new geographies defining
human social activity, the content of terminal examinations is the site of vehe-
ment debates and existential crises.

When it comes to the level of difficulty and the volume of knowledge
deemed necessary in examinations, standard setters tend to be influenced by
the global currency of knowledge. This explains why the level of mathematics and science required for Advanced Placement, A-levels, the International
Baccalaureate, and Matura systems — to name just a few — tends to be

similar. International assessments such as the Organisation for Economic Co-operation and Development [OECD]'s Pisa influence a global understanding of standards, leading to a type of pop-star ranking of countries whose scores are high and whom other countries hold up as models — Finland, China (Shanghai), Singapore, and Switzerland being examples.

The problem with this culture of convergence, equivalencies, and comparative epistemology is that it becomes difficult to stand back and forge something different. Instead, the temptation is to adopt and copy, often leading to cacophony, poor implementation, and curriculum overload as each national system tries to align with the next, which, indeed, will be seen as more rigorous. For Lines (2001), lack of acceptable rigour in examination processes is due to political reasons — as he puts it, because of the "determination of successive governments to centralize and control all aspects of education ... we have an examinations industry ... shorn of old standards and values, but required to serve increasing numbers of demanding customers" (p. 1).

This creates a type of global race to the top (perhaps we could call it a race to the bottom, if the "top" is holistic learning and the "bottom" is narrow, high-stakes performance). A few countries, like New Zealand, have designed competence frameworks for alternative assessment models (with more coursework, for example), but they are the exception to the rule.

Since universities have baseline prerequisites for admission, they influence standard setting in important ways, too. Although national examination boards set the examinations — and these boards take directives from education ministries, secretaries of education, regulatory frameworks, and/or associated bodies or councils — each university publishes admissions criteria for the admissions standards that it requires. Indeed, universities will not accept some national school-leaving certificates, such as a regular high-school certificate. This is sending out a signal to curriculum boards about the level of learning that universities exact.

State universities normally accept state-level high-school certification; for example, in Switzerland and France, state universities give automatic entrance to students who have passed the Matura or French Baccalaureate, respectively. However, selective and private universities might ask either for certain scores (in other words, passing state-level certification is not enough; students have to have done so to a certain degree of excellence) or a score on a separate placement test. In a globalised world where students might graduate from high school in one country but wish to pursue their studies in another, certificate recognition becomes even more critical and complex.

That examinations ultimately set the standard required for admission to university is hardly surprising and fits in with the overall structure of qualifications in the world of education: a string of vertically articulated requirements that, in theory, are increasingly rigorous, is needed for students to progress through school. In most systems, students must pass the year to progress to the next year; and, in many, students must pass examinations at the end of primary and middle school to be able to go to high school. Therefore, at the end of high school, an evaluation system is required for them to progress to the next level, which in most cases will be university. These series of qualification gateways proceed right through to the end of university (bachelor's, master's, doctorate). In some professions — such as in France, where most professions require an examination known as a "concours" — they continue within the profession itself, meaning that access to certain levels of employment can only be achieved if candidates pass further examinations.

Depending on the country, it is possible to find oneself in an entire culture of education and work governed by qualifications. At a broad sociological level this is understandable, as these qualifications vouch for the necessary competences to progress to a level of responsibility. It becomes crucial for professions such as airplane piloting, law, and medicine, to give just a few examples, where those eligible to practise have to have gone through rigorous tests of understanding and practice, which guarantee some level of quality and even security for the people who will be in their hands. However, this guarantee is based on the assumption that the qualifications are intrinsically representative of the skill, knowledge, and attitude needed for high performance in those professional areas. The nature of high-stakes testing rarely ensures this, creating instead a type of learning bulimia whereby teachers teach to the test, and students learn for test success rather than deep, conceptual understanding, appropriating by heart what they expect to see on the test and forgetting it soon after taking the examination.

Since many employers require university degrees, these degrees tend to carry much weight; hence, entry into universities is taken very seriously. Therefore, one could argue that out of all of these examinations, the end-of-high-school summative, narrow, and high-stakes assessments are the most critical since they are the tests that will open the door to eventual employment. Several statistics underline this, showing that high-school dropouts earn less than high-school graduates (NCES, 2017). Some employers will recognise and require the end-of-high-school certificate, although merely as a baseline.

Therefore, the two most powerful forces influencing the design of high-school assessment are nation-state political ideology, which has become globalised and intertwined with other nation-states at a macro level, and higher education, whose expectations set the tone for much examination setting.

1   **National Assessment Qualifications and University Recognition:**
         Politics and Networks

A pragmatic concern that has to be considered in the world of qualifications in general — but in particular when it comes to university acceptance of high-school certificate-bearing graduates — is demographics. Universities should be able to absorb the demand for places within a given country, and this dynamic will influence their admissions policies.

A 2014 study run by the European Parliament's Directorate-General for Internal Policies analysed university admissions dynamics across ten countries. The study found that university admissions systems had to adapt to three worldwide trends:

– The "capacity to absorb an ever increasing demand for higher education [...]" (the influential US Lumina Foundation [for example] set a 'Big Goal' of 60% of graduates by 2025 in the US)".
– "The expansion of the student population [...]. This expansion parallels a worldwide trend in the expansion of the private and for-profit sector, largely catering to a demand for higher education that the public system cannot accommodate".
– "The increasing mobility of students". (European Parliament, 2014, p. 15)

This creates a complex dynamic whereby universities must create places for incoming students while maintaining a high standard of admissions. Whether they truly create spaces or not is another discussion. In many continental European universities, undergraduate programmes tend to be overpopulated. The level of study in bachelor's programmes is very high, causing high attrition and culling the student population down to a more manageable size at honours- and master's-programme levels. Many private and competitive universities have responded by simply accepting fewer students. Studies have shown, for example, that Ivy League colleges have not expanded their student populations over the past decades despite quantum leaps in demand (Blair & Smetters, 2021).

In this context of increased pressure and competition, the European Parliament study (2014) showed that high-school tests, as opposed to grade averages, were the "least reliable" predictors of university success (p. 72). Demographically, without widespread reform of both the nature of university admissions testing and the management of demand by a substantive increase in supply, the chokehold will merely get worse, putting young people in situations where the prospect of graduating from university with qualifications is ever more distant and difficult to obtain.

Another problem concerning the end-of-high-school examination-based assessment as a gateway to higher education is human error — a staple of the world of assessment — from rater bias to problems of construct validity in curriculum design, to simple technical errors and mismanagement of the colossal logistical operation of marking millions of examinations across the world every year.

Issacs and Gorgen (2018) point out that examination systems undergo regular crises because of human error. One example is the "Scottish examinations in 2000, in which over 5,000 potentially university bound students ostensibly received incomplete or inaccurate results" (p. 316); another is the rushed standards-setting in the UK in 2000, the results of which meant that "more than 90,000 examinations were re-marked, and although most did not result in overall A level qualification grade changes, over 100 students initially missed out on their university places" (p. 316).

While national curriculum boards might be responsible for setting university entrance examinations and also for setting standards at the end of national high school, various case studies from around the world have shown that many universities will create their own selection process in spite of this:

> Competitive university programmes sometimes either imposed additional requirements alongside those needed for general entry or they specified courses that applicants should take while in upper secondary. Some universities delayed selection to competitive programmes until a student's second year of university so that they could use results from the first year in the decision making process. (Isaacs & Gorgen, p. 324)

All of this accentuates the valency, risk, and pressure associated with the end-of-high-school summative assessment. Examinations in the lower levels of school are less frequent, most probably because the playing field is less political. A 2023 OECD study on student assessment showed:

> Across the 39 countries and other participants in this study, less than half have any national/central examinations at primary and lower secondary levels (3 at primary level and 14 at lower secondary level), but 34 have at least one at upper secondary level (in general programmes).

As forthcoming chapters of this book will show, the model of assessment used in many primary, middle, and lower secondary schools is, in many ways, more valid, ecological, and life-worthy, precisely because it has not been skewed by excessive exogenic pressure.

2 University Recognition of Different Diplomas

2.1 *UCAS Tariff Tables*

The university-acceptance model in the United Kingdom is an interesting approach to analyse in the light of pitfalls, pressures, and cultural biases. The University and Colleges Admissions Service (UCAS), created in 1993, converts different diploma scores (England, Scotland, International Baccalaureate, etc.) into a points system. These points are then used as entry "tariffs" to university. Students need to gain a certain number of points to be eligible for entry to certain universities. This can be a controversial exercise since some subjective judgement comes into play when comparing different end-of-high-school systems.

Because the UCAS system is British, the points system tends to lean in favour of a British approach to high school, which is narrow and specialised rather than broad based. As such, students who graduate with a broad-based curriculum — such as the International Baccalaureate Diploma Programme (IBDP) — which is designed to create a holistic learning experience (six subjects, an extended essay, theory of knowledge, creativity, activity, and service learning), see the IBDP converted in such a way that the pressure is to achieve a certain number of points in certain subjects rather than broad achievement across the board. Whereas students graduating with A-levels may gain places having studied three or four subjects, IBDP students might be able to gain the same level of recognition but will have to have studied many more subjects to get there.

2.2 *Swiss Universities and International Qualifications*

Swiss universities accept the national Matura qualification, asking only that students pass it to be admitted. However, students who have earned an International Baccalaureate Diploma must gain a certain number of points and will only be accepted if they have studied certain subjects; art, theory of knowledge, and various humanities are not recognised. This narrows the experience of those studying the IBDP, essentially skewing it into a different type of diploma.

2.3 *North America: Standardised Admissions Testing and Test-Optional Colleges*

North American universities operate differently than most European universities, quite often by setting entry qualifications over and above school-leaving certificates. Because the high-school diploma in the United States is not externally examined, standards cannot be monitored. Therefore, above a certain grade average, universities will ask students to sit a placement test, either the SAT (originally known as the Scholastic Aptitude Test, developed as an IQ test in the Army in the 1920s and later expanded to universities as a placement test

[*Manhattan Review*, 2023]) or the ACT (invented in 1959 and enhanced in the 1980s [*Manhattan Review*, 2023]).

Most competitive universities prefer students who have graduated with Advanced Placement examinations or an International Baccalaureate. During and after the Covid-19 pandemic, a number of universities went "test optional", meaning that they no longer required a placement test but instead asked for a grade average over the past four years of study. This corresponds to research done by the European Parliament that grade averages are more reliable predictors of student performance than examination scores (2014, p. 15).

North American universities tend to be interested in students' nonacademic achievements — such as their involvement in arts, sports, leadership, advocacy, community service, and social impact work. The personal statement is an important part of the selection process and sends out a signal that the university is seeking more than high-stakes, narrow test performances. In many ways, this cultural approach to university entrance is more in line with the type of forward-looking, holistic appreciation of students' learning needed for individual flourishing, social renewal, and a more inclusive understanding of what it means to be educated.

2.4   *India: The Extremities of Meritocracy*

University entrance acceptance in India is highly competitive, taken to extremes when it comes to the prestigious institutes of technology, of which there are only 23 for more than 1.4 billion people. As a result, higher-education admissions rates are very low for the more competitive colleges. Thousands of students prepare for entrance tests each year, often by signing up for special coaching colleges whose sole purpose is to prepare students for the entrance examinations, the most famous being in the city of Kota (Kale, 2018).

The pressure to perform has led to a string of student suicides: over 45 between 2014 and 2017; in 2018, "more than 20 students in one Indian state committed suicide due to failed university admission exams" (Wallen, 2019).

The extremity of this situation puts into question not only the nature of university placement testing but also the number of institutions available for students to attend and the side effects of this scarcity principle.

3   Releasing the Chokehold

National curriculum and examination-setting organisations working within a globally competitive framework influence the style and content of high-school assessment. In tandem with universities — whose entrance requirements range from placement tests to accepting national diplomas in a less-stringent fashion than international diplomas — they have put any chance of reform in a chokehold.

In order to break out of this, courage and collaboration will be needed.

References

Alvarez, B. (2023). Florida's new history standard: "A blow to our students and nation". *NEA Today*. https://www.nea.org/nea-today/all-news-articles/floridas-new-history-standard-blow-our-students-and-nation

Blair, P. Q., & Smetters, K. (2021). *Why don't elite colleges expand supply?* Working paper 29309. National Bureau of Economic Research. https://www.nber.org/system/files/working_papers/w29309/w29309.pdf

European Parliament. (2014). *Higher education entrance qualifications and exams in Europe: A comparison*. Directorate General for Internal Policies. European Union.

Isaacs, T., & Gogen, K. (2018). Culture, context and controversy in setting national examination standards. In J. Baird, T. Isaacs, D. Opposs, & L. Grey (Eds.), *Examination standards: How measures and meanings differ around the world*. IOE Press.

Kale, S. (2018, April 20). In India, high-pressure exams are creating a student suicide crisis. *WIRED*. https://www.wired.co.uk/article/india-kota-student-suicide-exams-institutes-of-technology

Lines, D. (2000, April 7). A disaster waiting to happen. *Times Educational Supplement*.

Manhattan Review (2023). *SAT prep: SAT history*. https://www.manhattanreview.com/sat-history/

NCES [National Center for Education Statistics]. (2017). *Trends in high school dropout and completion rates in the United States*. https://nces.ed.gov/programs/dropout/index.asp

OECD [Organisation for Economic Co-operation and Development]. (2023). *Student assessment*. https://gpseducation.oecd.org/revieweducationpolicies/#!node=41738&filter=all

Wallen, J. (2019). Over twenty Indian students commit suicide after inaccurate university admission results. *Telegraph*. https://www.telegraph.co.uk/news/2019/04/30/twenty-indian-students-commit-suicide-inaccurate-university/

CHAPTER 7

Primary- and Middle-School Models

In seeking to dynamise and reform the end-of-high-school assessment, one can consider several models. Before going beyond familiar territory, we should look at what happens lower down in the school. The penetrating insights of several famous researchers in child development and cognition — Piaget, Vygotsky, Montessori, Freinet, Froebel, and Bloom, resuscitated and actualised by Bruner, Perkins, and Gardner — currently form the premises of primary education, and should be used as much as possible in high-school education. This is mainly because their emphasis is on the intricacies of social and emotional learning, formative assessment, and learning itself rather than on performance. However, despite what we know about learning from psychological, sociological, and increasingly neurobiological perspectives, these progressive pedagogic models tend not to migrate from primary school up to high school.

A pedagogical vision focusing on holistic development has flourished in primary grades over time — almost certainly because the Damoclean sword of high-stakes, narrow assessment does not hang over primary years with the same ominous presence that it does over high-school years. Once educators have been released from the pressure to perform and to put students through the testing regime that consumes all of the students' and the teachers' focus and energy, there is much more oxygen for creativity, discussion, critical thinking, and progress in deep learning. This is why a simple walk through most primary schools is a journey into playfulness, joy, art, and community.

Therefore, one way of improving the experience of upper high school could be to look to much of the pedagogy of primary schooling and to expand and develop it in secondary schooling. This is a question of form rather than content: the argument is not that the academic level of primary schooling should be duplicated in high school, more the teaching style. This happens, to a certain extent, in some middle and lower high schools (12- to 15-year-olds) but rarely, if at all, in the senior years of school.

1   Inquiry-Based Learning

The pedagogic revolutions of the early 1900s, driven by Piaget, Vygotsky, Montessori, and Dewey, had a number of points in common. The psychology of learning, more than the content of transmission, became a focus: the

understanding that language development is central in learning and that creative task-design can bring out much richer learning than medieval didacticism
and catechistic methods. On this last point, theorists and educators, particularly Montessori, recognised the role of curiosity as a driver in the process of
learning.

These thinkers were all influenced by the visionary, polemical, contradic-
tory but brilliant Swiss philosopher Jean-Jacques Rousseau. His foundational
text, *Emile ou Sur L'éducation* (published in 1762), put forward a thesis that
essentially deconstructed transmission models altogether, placing the student
in a position of natural inquiry where she or he would find responses through a
type of Platonic inner reasoning, with the teacher providing minimally invasive
prompts and scaffolds. Examples from the Enlightenment text express well the
spirit of inquiry-based learning: "[W]ith our foolish and pedantic methods"
[says Rousseau] "we are always preventing children from learning what they
could learn much better by themselves" (Rousseau, 2024).

Rousseau argues that a natural environment often provides a better stage
for learning than an excessively contrived tutorial:

> Nature provides for the child's growth in her own fashion, and this should
> never be thwarted. Do not make him sit still when he wants to run about,
> nor run when he wants to be quiet. If we did not spoil our children's
> wills by our blunders their desires would be free from caprice. Let them
> run, jump, and shout to their heart's content. All their own activities are
> instincts of the body for the growth in strength; but you should regard
> with suspicion those wishes which they cannot carry out for themselves,
> those which others must carry out for them. (*Émile,* Book 2)

At face value, this naturalistic assumption might seem more philosophically
than scientifically based, but increasing research in learning through play and
the importance of a natural environment for student wellbeing and learning
shows that Rousseau was ahead of his time (Mader, 2022).

More recent iterations of this line of thinking, henceforth called "inquiry-
based learning", were elaborated by Schwab from the University of Chicago
in the 1960s, pointing to classroom and task design that would allow students
more choice in their activities. The idea was that in exercising this autonomy
and volition, more creative, critical, and socially productive learning would
take place. In his 1960 paper "Inquiry, the Science Teacher, and the Educator", Schwab clearly had senior students in mind. However, today, the spirit of
inquiry-based learning barely exists at the very end of high school.[1]

Some primary programmes, such as the International Baccalaureate's Primary Years Programme (PYP), exemplify many of the principles of

inquiry-based learning: students learn units of inquiry that allow them to "use their initiative to take responsibility and ownership of their learning" (International Baccalaureate, 2024.) The end-of-cycle assessment, called the "PYP exhibition", includes many core features of inquiry-based learning: it "involves students working collaboratively to conduct an in-depth inquiry into a real-life issue or problem that's pertinent to them" (Southbank International School, 2024).

Needless to say, an environment marked by highly pressurised cramming for examinations, characteristic of secondary schools, is a far cry from this vision. Although students might be involved in exhibitions and inquiry-styled pedagogy in classrooms, the nature of high-stakes testing at the end of high school severely interrupts this. Interestingly, a study conducted by Toe and colleagues (2016) on assessment in the PYP revealed that, even in the primary years, despite the programme's intention to focus on learning and discovery, parent expectations could push schools to be more test-centric and, therefore, less inquiry-focussed. They wrote, in that study: "Some tensions were observed between mandated external standardised testing and assessment approaches, particularly formative approaches developed within the school. Tensions can emerge when parents place high value upon these test results" (p. 111).

2 Project-Based Learning

Project-based learning (PBL) is another staple of primary and middle schools of which there is less and less as students approach the end of high school. The notion, rooted in Dewey's ideas, is that students engage in independent or quasi-independent inquiry, with minimal teacher scaffolds, in order to solve a problem or conduct an investigation or study. Projects tend to be extended pieces of work and culminate in some product: a presentation, work of art, model, or extended piece of writing. Zhang and Ma's 2023 study on the impact of PBL on secondary-school students' literacy showed that "compared with the traditional teaching model, project-based learning significantly improved students' learning outcomes and positively contributed to academic achievement, affective attitudes, and thinking skills, especially academic achievement" (p. 1). Other studies have shown benefits in primary education, too (Kaldi, Filippatou, & Govaris, 2011).

Some educators have criticised PBL, however, on a number of fronts: for the paucity of research on its real impact; for the lack of structure it provides students with learning needs; and, some studies suggest, for being bad for learning (Miller & Krajcik, 2019). A now famous 2006 article by Kirschner, Sweller, and Clark essentially ripped apart not only PBL but also inquiry-based learning, discovery learning, and even constructivism (that is, the idea that knowledge is built up by students, with the teacher as a co-learner). This led to two responses (Hmelo-Silver et al., 2007; Schmidt et al., 2007) and a response to the responses (Sweller et al., 2007). The crux of the quarrel was weighing cognitive-load theory (arguing that given the comparative weakness of working memory, instruction has to be chunked and scaffolded) against inquiry-based learning (where teachers intervene comparatively little, and students are given much more space to learn by themselves).

A strong argument for projects is that they tend to mirror the world of work much more closely than do traditional declarative knowledge tests. Projects habituate students to apply themselves to longer assignments involving research, very much the way employers structure many workplace assignments.

Of course, like so many pedagogical theories, implementation is the decisive factor since classroom environments depend largely on how deeply the teacher is committed to learning happening, regardless of the method. The problem, from this book's perspective, is more that PBL's benefits (as disputed as they might be) cannot flourish in an environment where there is no time for projects because students have to spend classroom time not discovering new knowledge but preparing for tests.

It is unusual for students to engage in projects in the final year of high school: what might resemble projects will be coursework or internal assessments, which tend to be academic pieces that will contribute to students' overall end-of-school grade. If students did projects instead of at least some final examinations, with a less aggressive summative assessment component, it would arguably be a more mindful, holistic, and valid way of assessing not only their knowledge and skills but also their approaches to learning.

3   Creativity

At the deepest level, the atmosphere created in primary classrooms allows for a greater level of creativity than the examination-charged climate at the end of high school. This is partly because the arts usually play a major role in primary education but feature less and less prominently as students make their way up the various year levels, until they reach the end of school. In the UK, over the last decades a clear decline has occurred in the number of creative subjects (such as the arts) that students choose (#Save Our Subjects, 2024; Morrison, 2019), and the trend is similar in the United States. To give an example, a 2022 census in New Jersey showed that while 96%

of elementary-school students and 89% of middle-school students actively participated in the arts, only 50% of high-school students did (Morrison et al., 2022).

This is despite the fact that exposure to the arts is good for overall academic achievement (Egana-del Sol, 2023); further, the arts create a platform for students to express themselves and develop their creativity. The pattern of a steady diminishment of creative activities for children as they approach the end of high school[2] is not restricted to the formal curriculum: often children will enrol in such extracurricular activities as ballet, music, pottery, and theatre at a young age, but, as end-of-high-school examinations become more imminent, these activities drop off and the focus becomes steadily and resolutely fixed on examination performance.

It is understandable that this is what happens given the weighting of examinations and the overall importance they signify for high-school graduation. Arts subjects are almost never mandated for high-school certification the way that mathematics or languages are. Although a US-styled high-school diploma requires credits in the arts, far fewer credits are needed for the arts than for other subject areas — allowing students to discontinue their study of the arts in the final two years of school, if not earlier.

When a curriculum offers arts subjects, fewer students take them than other subjects. For example, out of the 679,741 candidates who sat IB Diploma examinations in May 2023, only 27,509 registered for the arts (International Baccalaureate, 2023). Although the arts are booming as an industry, many parents and students see greater value in subjects like business management and pure sciences, since they are still perceived as having higher status. If there was less inordinate pressure on students to do well in STEM subjects above others, a greater curriculum balance would no doubt be struck.

4   Rest, Pacing, and Wellbeing

One of the joys of primary schools is the mindful pace of learning. Students often engage in outdoor learning; there are naps, storytelling, circle time, and games to punctuate the rhythm of student socialisation and competence development.

These types of activity, which centre wellbeing, tend to grind to a halt as students approach the end of high-school examination period. At the same time, levels of anxiety and mental illness are at an all-time high among high-school students (Cain Miller, 2024; Campbell, 2024).

As our understanding increases concerning the importance of sleep for health, mental acuity, wellbeing, and general productivity, the calls are growing louder for high school to start later in the day (APA, 2023). The reason adolescents would function better later in the day is that they are not getting enough sleep — in part, because they are up all night revising for examinations. "Excessive revision and its effect on sleep patterns can have serious repercussions both mentally and physiologically [...]. According to the UK Sleep Council, in the month prior to exams, more than 80 percent of teens said their sleep was affected by stress and pre-exam nerves" (Webster, 2018). By following a more flexible week, timetabled as in primary schools, students would probably get more sleep and be healthier.

If the checkerboard of summative high-stakes assessments were dismantled, something far more ecological, student-friendly, mindful, and creativity-inducing would have to be put in its place — a system that would take into account what it means to be a young person in the twenty-first century, with daunting challenges and difficult prospects regarding the future world and environment of work. If the stakes at the end of the journey cast less of a shadow over the pathway leading up to it, there would be more time and space for a primary-school-styled learning environment.

5   Why Do These Models Not Transfer into Secondary Schools?

Some high schools have looked at alternative models, and we will explore those in the next chapters of this book. However, most high schools have very little in common with primary schools, especially in the last year or two of instruction.

Thinkers of the early twentieth century who designed theories of education that put the emphasis on pedagogy and learning rather than on performance, were including all kinds of learners. However, with the intensification of testing in secondary schools, educators struggle to implement these theories fully. This is fundamentally because the culture of testing has made it difficult if not impossible to create the conditions for genuine learning that the constructivists had in mind. Post-constructivist thinkers like David Perkins and Howard Gardner have been pointing this out for decades.

As global competition for university places increases, without an intentional and concerted effort to change the assessment paradigm, it is less likely than ever that the spirit of primary learning will influence high-school classrooms. Worse, in some contexts, such as in the UK, the checkerboard of high-school–styled assessment has entered the primary school, creating a test-obsessed learning climate and actually reversing the situation, crowding out inquiry-based learning in favour of cramming.

If we do not do something about it, the testing-over-learning paradigm might take over the whole arc of schooling, leaving an enclave of wellbeing and anxiety-free pedagogy in just the kindergarten and early years.

This is why we need to take a whole-school approach to assessment, with an understanding of the vertical articulation of learning outcomes from the early years all the way up to the end of high school.

Notes

1   It is, however, true that a spirit of inquiry has subsequently been developed through experimentation in many high-school science classrooms. However, when it comes to end-of-school examinations in science, a written examination supersedes the creative thinking and doing associated with laboratory work; any inquiry-based work that has been allowed to exist features in the form of graded coursework. Since this coursework *is* graded, its assessment thwarts the psychological safety that should arise in grade-free inquiry-based work, making the exercise a type of internal examination rather than a genuine exploration freed from grade anxiety.

2   This is a generalisation rather than a hard fact, but I think nonetheless a fair generalisation.

References

APA [American Psychological Association]. (2023). *Later school times promote adolescent well-being.* https://www.apa.org/topics/children/school-start-times

Cain Miller, C. (2024, January 1). Today's teenagers: Anxious about their futures and disillusioned by politicians. *New York Times.* https://www.nytimes.com/2024/01/29/upshot/teens-politics-mental-health.html

Campbell, D. (2024, February 2). Nearly a third of UK secondary pupils avoid school due to anxiety, survey finds. *The Guardian.* https://www.theguardian.com/society/2024/feb/02/almost-three-in-10-secondary-pupils-in-uk-avoiding-school-because-of-anxiety

Egana-del Sol, P. (2023). The impacts of a high-school art-based program on academic achievements, creativity, and creative behaviors. *NPJ Science of Learning, 8*(39). https://doi.org/10.1038/s41539-023-00187-6

Hmelo-Silver, C. E., Duncan, R. G., & Chinn, C. A. (2007). Scaffolding and achievement in problem-based and inquiry learning: A response to Kirschner, Sweller, and Clark (2006). *Educational Psychologist, 42*(2), 99–107.

International Baccalaureate. (2023). *The IB Diploma programme and career-related programme final statistical bulletin: May 2023 assessment session.* https://www.ibo.org/globalassets/new-structure/about-the-ib/pdfs/dp-cp-final-statistical-bulletin-may-2023.pdf

International Baccalaureate. (2024). *Primary years programme.* https://www.ibo.org/programmes/primary-years-programme/

Kaldi, S., Filippatou, D., & Govaris, C. (2011). Project-based learning in primary schools: Effects on pupils' learning and attitudes. *Education 3–13, 39*(1), 35–47. https://doi.org/10.1080/03004270903179538

Kirschner, P. A., Sweller, J., & Clark, R. E. (2006). Why minimal guidance during instruction does not work: An analysis of the failure of constructivist, discovery, problem-based, experiential, and inquiry-based teaching. *Educational Psychologist, 41*(2), 75–86. https://doi.org/10.1207/s15326985ep4102_1

Mader, J. (2022, November 14). Want resilient and well-adjusted kids? Let them play. *Hechinger Report.* https://hechingerreport.org/want-resilient-and-well-adjusted-kids-let-them-play/

Miller, E. C., & Krajcik, J. S. (2019). Promoting deep learning through project-based learning: A design problem. *Disciplinary and Interdisciplinary Science Education Research, 1*(7). https://doi.org/10.1186/s43031-019-0009-6

Morrison, N. (2019, April 9). How the arts are being squeezed out of schools. *Forbes.* https://www.forbes.com/sites/nickmorrison/2019/04/09/how-the-arts-are-being-squeezed-out-of-schools/

Morrison, R. B., Young, A., Cirillo, P. (2022). The resilience of arts ed now: Beyond the pandemic. *The 2021 New Jersey Arts Education Census Project Report.* Quadrant Research.

Rousseau, J. J. (2024). Émile, *ou De l'éducation* [Émile, or On education]. Petites Classiques Larousse. [Originally published 1762]. https://edtechbooks.org/philosophy_of_education/emile_2

Save Our Subjects. (2024). *Save our subjects: A campaign for broadening the curriculum.* https://www.saveoursubjects.org/

Schmidt, H. G., Loyens, S. M. M., van Gog, T., & Paas, F. (2007). Problem-based learning is compatible with human cognitive architecture: Commentary on Kirschner, Sweller, and Clark (2006). *Educational Psychologist, 42*(2), 91–97.

Schwab, J. (1960). Inquiry, the science teacher, and the educator. *The School Review, 68*(2). https://www.journals.uchicago.edu/doi/10.1086/442536

Southbank International School. (2024). *PYP exhibition.* https://www.southbank.org/primary-years-programme/exhibition/

Sweller, J., Kirschner, P., & Clark, R. (2007). Why minimally guided teaching techniques do not work: A reply to commentaries. *Educational Psychologist, 42*(2), 115–121. https://doi.org/10.1080/00461520701263426

Toe, D., Lang, J., Paatsch, L., Yim, B., Jobling, W., Doig, B., & Aranda, G. (2016). *Assessment of student development and learning in International Baccalaureate Primary Years Programme schools.* International Baccalaureate Organization.

Webster, N. (2018, June 10). Lack of sleep during stressful exams has "serious repercussions for pupils". *The National News.* https://www.thenationalnews.com/uae/lack-of-sleep-during-stressful-exams-has-serious-repercussions-for-pupils-1.738554

Zhang, L., & Ma, Y. (2023). A study of the impact of project-based learning on student learning effects: A meta-analysis study. *Frontiers in Psychology, 14.* https://doi.org/10.3389/fpsyg.2023.1202728

CHAPTER 8

Alternative High-School Models

While primary- and middle-school models might offer a viable substitute to summative, high-stakes assessment at the end of high school, a number of alternative programmes are available to students throughout the world. Not all of these necessarily mitigate the problems we have identified with examination-based assessments, but most tend to be less centred on testing and several allow for the recognition of nonacademic learning and achievement.

Some of these alternative programmes, such as vocational courses, have been in place for several decades. It is the cultural tradition in some countries, such as Switzerland and Germany, to not only provide nonacademic pathways for students but also to promote these pathways — with the result that they are more popular and more in demand than traditional academic programmes. Other efforts to widen assessment are more recent and in some cases are still in an experimental phase. What all of these programmes have in common is that they offer different routes to the end of high school and beyond, bringing hope to the project to make assessment more diverse, broad based, and inclusive.

However, a major problem is that universities do not recognise several of the alternative transcripts from these nontraditional programmes, even though they reflect many of the competences that universities are seeking in students. For the chokehold of high-stakes summative assessments to be released and for the checkerboard of standardised, narrow testing to give way to assessments based on a more pluralistic and inclusive appreciation of student learning, these alternative systems will have to be recognised more fulsomely across the globe.

1 Vocational Programmes

The tradition of vocational studies is longstanding and can be traced back to the origins of formal education itself in that the practical application of knowledge in a work setting was the staple of many ancient learning paradigms. In circa 425 BCE, Herodotus wrote of the Persians as, from "ages five to twenty years, [being] trained in horsemanship, archery, and telling the truth" (2003, book 1, p. 136).

© UNESCO IBE, 2025 | DOI:10.1163/9789004714205_008

With the industrial revolution of the 1800s, philosophers started to notice the discrepancy between a highly academic education still heavily ensconced in the catechistic tradition of the Middle Ages, and the need for more practical, hands-on learning. The explosion of the arts during the Renaissance and the sciences during the Enlightenment had changed work, research, and the overall distribution of knowledge. These changes raised the question of whether the education most students experienced was preparing them for the world and to what extent it should be adapted to new realities. This issue informed the thinking of Wilhelm von Humboldt and Friedrich Froebel, two important figures in the development of the German school of educational philosophy.

Indeed, as an indirect consequence of their work, vocational education in Germany — known as the vocational education and training system (VET) — grew quickly. This involves a dual structure whereby students move between theoretical classes and on-site apprenticeships. Similar models have arisen in Switzerland and Austria.

In Switzerland, the apprenticeship model is extremely popular: "[M]ore than 90% of young people [...] earn a school or apprenticeship certificate after completing upper secondary (post-compulsory) education" (SWI, 2024). Importantly, flexibility has been built into the model, so that students may enrol in more academic studies after their apprenticeship if they change their mind about the pathway they wish to take. One reason that the vocational stream is more popular than a traditional academic course is because it offers a high probability of employment in well-remunerated professions.

In the UK, where the predominant high-school qualifications are A-levels, in 2020 the government introduced what are known as "T-levels" (technical qualifications). These qualifications come through a B-TEC course, which involves practical, hands-on experience. These technical qualifications are worth tariff points on the UCAS table,[1] making them theoretically equivalent to the more academic A-levels.

Although vocational courses offer an alternative to traditional end-of-high-school qualifications, the assessment system that characterises them is not necessarily as forward looking as one might hope. In some cases, test-bound academic qualifications are still required; and in most cases, vocational qualifications are awarded after an examination.

This is not to say that examinations per se are a problematic way of assessing students; much depends on the manner in which the examinations are designed and exactly what type of competence they are testing. However, the importance conferred on these tests does remind us that the predominant assumption in the world of qualifications is that an *examination* will best describe the knowledge, attitude, and skills gleaned over a course of study — which is clearly not always the case.

Despite all of this, vocational courses offer a viable alternative to students completing high school and open a pathway that allows different types of skills to flourish than those tested in traditional high-stakes assessments.

2   Microcredentialing and Digital Badges

Microcredentials are short units of study, lasting roughly one to twelve weeks each. Rather than offering learning in long units, as is the case with academic courses, they allow students to focus on precise modules and to stack these in credits (Hess, 2023). These credits can be aggregated to give students the equivalent of a degree or a recognised certificate. At the time of writing, a number of higher-education establishments (e.g., the universities of Melbourne, Kent, and Glasgow) offered microcredentials.

Two arguments for microcredentials are that they allow far more flexibility than traditional courses and are more affordable than traditional academic pathways. However, their focus tends to be market-driven, with a utilitarian approach to learning that makes it as efficient as possible but also, potentially, as narrow as possible. Furthermore, the sized-down dimension of microlearning in general does not necessarily remove the problem of its assessment being excessively high stakes. However, the resulting assessment-heaviness is eased by not having an entire cursus bundled in one set of end-of-year examinations, but instead having shorter tasks mark a series of learning experiences.

Microcredentialing tends to be offered at the (university) undergraduate level rather than at the high-school level. However, as it becomes more recognised at university level, its potential eligibility as a high-school certification becomes easier to envisage. In order for universities to recognise microcredentials, it would take an innovative and courageous effort of a coalition of high schools to trial them instead of continuing with regular academic courses only.

"Digital badging" is similar to microcredentialing in that it consists of awarding credit for shorter episodes that are more diverse and flexible in nature than traditional academic courses. The main difference is that digital badges are broader in what they recognise, ranging from sports awards to business achievements. By being digital, this type of credentialing is particularly broad and far-reaching and has the potential to disrupt traditional certification schemes profoundly. For badging to be effective, it needs to be part of the "exchange system" of a consortium that has agreed on what constitutes sufficient merit to earn a badge and what the comparative value of the badge is — allowing for a harmonised and regulated currency.

This system of recognition goes back to the early 2000s. Since then, open-source companies such as Mozilla have developed it substantially. Not unlike other disruptive technologies, including cryptocurrencies, digital badging has been criticised regarding its validity and robustness (Detroja et al., 2017).

Until such time as digital badging has become widely recognised and para-metrised within a larger educational-equivalencies model, it will continue to evolve on the fringes of mainstream assessment regimes. Were it to be embraced and deployed more widely, it would allow far greater access to cer-tification than the current model, which excludes many students because of cost and accessibility. Indeed, using assessment based on digital badging would open up the real possibility that students from around the world — including those living in poverty — would have their skills recognised and validated.

3   Alternative Transcripts

Traditional transcripts are important documents for students graduating from high school. Universities and other post-secondary institutions look to these for baseline entry requirement data, especially in North America and coun-tries that use a North American–styled academic-recognition approach. A number of different end-of-high-school certificates exist, such as the Inter-national Baccalaureate; British A-levels; the China High School Academic Proficiency Test (Huikao); the Japanese Upper Secondary School Graduation Certificate (Kotogakko Sotsugyo Shosho); the Indian Senior School Certificate, Pre-University Certificate, and Pre-Degree Certificate; the French Baccalaure-ate; Swiss and Italian Matura; and the German Arbitur. In the UK and many European countries, many universities will only accept a programme diploma; whereas, in the United States, all universities will accept high-school diplomas based on achievement during the last four years of school (sometimes two), normally with a university placement test alongside. So-called top-tier univer-sities prefer a certificate or diploma on top of the high-school diploma.

What all of these certifications have in common is that they are narrow in scope (testing academic proficiency) and high stakes in valency (representing a gateway to future prospects). Not all institutions are willing to go no further than the traditional model of the end-of-high-school assessment, and a num-ber of alternative transcripts are used across a variety of schools. Alternative transcripts look to supplement or even replace classical academic grade tran-scripts with evaluation systems that describe a broader range of skills, knowl-edge, and dispositions.

3.1   *The Global Citizenship Diploma (GCD)*

The Yokohama International School established the Global Citizenship Diploma (GCD) in 2011. Nine schools across the world, mainly international ones, now use this diploma. It awards three levels of recognition — certificate, diploma, and diploma with distinction — that honour: (1) commitment to the values of global citizenship (understanding of others, action, and advocacy), (2) evidence of learning in a set number of competencies (academics, academic skills, advanced academics, public communications, community skills, artistic expression, wellness, leadership, global understanding, management, wilderness engagement, multilingualism, intercultural communication, personal goals, work experience, and personal accomplishments), and (3) achievement in "areas of expertise" (GCD, n.d.).

While the intention behind this diploma is to move away from traditional end-of-high-school assessments, the structure is fairly hierarchical — essentially, awarding, above others, students who have stacked the greatest number of competencies and achievements. Further, the definition of "competencies" is not altogether clear: why, for example, are there three different competencies related to academics? In addition, it is unclear if universities and/or employers accept or recognise the GCD, a problem most alternative transcripts face.

Nonetheless, the GCD is a bold attempt to rethink the end of high school and the types of qualities that a school should be celebrating in its graduates.

3.2   *The Mastery Transcript Consortium (MTC)*

The headmaster of Hawken School, a private school in Ohio, founded the Mastery Transcript Consortium (MTC) in 2017. It has since grown into the company that it is today, which seeks to have schools use the MTC model to present student learning through competencies. Whereas the Global Citizenship Diploma describes a number of competencies, the MTC leaves it up to member schools to decide what they understand by a competency. Students graduate with a transcript that describes the skills they have developed at high school, irrespective of their academic diploma qualifications.

Schools who join the consortium are expected to use the digital platform designed by the company to describe these competencies to universities or employers. A strong feature of the MTC is that competencies are not graded: "MTC members don't reduce learners to single numbers, but they do hold them to high standards. When learners master critical skills and content, they earn competencies which combine to create a clear, succinct visualization of each learner's strengths" (MTC, 2021).

At the time of writing, the MTC claimed that 433 institutions accepted their alternative transcript. It is not clear if this is in lieu of a standard grade transcript or alongside it as an extra piece of admissions information.

MTC's advantage is that it is a well-developed company with a board and strong communication resources, which means that it can make a considerable impact. Its disadvantages are that it is a commercial product with a fee, meaning that some schools might not be able to afford it; and that competencies are not clearly defined and will therefore differ from one establishment to the next, not offering any overarching, cohesive definition of what a competency is.

The main challenge that alternative transcripts like the GCD and MTC have is breaking into the territory of higher-education recognition and having universities, colleges, and even employers appreciate their value. Since the currency of established academic transcripts and school completion certification is very strong, most institutions that show interest in these alternatives do so only as an addition to the standard requirements. Furthermore, the institutions that are prepared to do this tend to be concentrated in the United States: very few, if any, UK, Swiss, or Dutch universities will accept alternative transcripts.

4 Creative School-Based Projects

There is a plethora of school-based projects with, as a common goal, the enhancement of more holistic and creative ways of assessing student learning. Most of these are in private, international, or independent schools. The following are particularly innovative examples.

4.1 The UWCA Systems Transformation Pathway

On its website, the United World College of the Atlantic (UWCA), the first of the United World colleges, founded by Kurth Hahn, describe this programme in the following words:

> The Systems Transformation Pathway is fundamentally action-oriented, it replaces written exams and classroom-based learning with relevant, ambitious, necessary work in complex and authentic real-world contexts. This course equips students to go beyond treating symptoms to advance transformative change at a systems level. To be effective at this, students will benefit from understanding and apprenticing themselves to systems in a specific impact area — food, biodiversity, energy, or migration. (UWCA, n.d.)

Students are able to substitute some of the academic subjects of their International Baccalaureate (IB) diploma with modules in systems transformation. This leads to hands-on work and "self-directed intervention" in the student's home environment. There is a "festival showcase" of learning at the end of the process.

By using the IB as the curriculum framework in which the systems transformation takes place, UWCA is allowing its students to explore a different model of learning from the traditional academic approach and yet have this recognised by post-secondary institutions who accept the IB as a qualification.

4.2   *HoloTracker*

HoloTracker, designed by a Singaporian company, is an example of how technology can enhance alternative assessment systems. Teachers enter feedback on the fly into an electronic portal that generates clusters of recognition in areas of social and human development. The areas mapped are virtues, inquiry, empathy, effectiveness, cognition, and being (HoloTracker, 2023). If several comments are made in one area of a student's learning, this cluster is reinforced.

An advantage with this type of assessment tool is that it allows for ongoing assessment rather than waiting till the end of a cycle and going through the somewhat contrived business of bunching evaluations in short, concentrated bursts of information. The fact that assessment is steady and ongoing relieves pressure on students and in many ways increases validity, allowing for a more distributed and paced appreciation of learning. A weak point is the defined areas, since these are either too generic ("being") or unclear ("effectiveness"). Deciding on a student's virtue is also problematic in regard to assessment validity, reliability, and fairness — as the whole construct of "virtue" is not universally understood in the same manner.

4.3   *Amala*

Set up in 2017 in collaboration with the United World College of South East Asia, Amala's purpose is to provide refugees with an education and school-leaving certification: the Amala Global Secondary Diploma and "Changemaker Courses" in Peace-building, Ethical Leadership, and Social Entrepreneurship (Amala, 2024).

Courses are either in person or online and take place across the world. On its website, Amala explains:

> [T]here are no exams, rather, throughout the programme, students provide evidence of their learning in order to meet Amala's seven key

competency areas: sustainable innovation, resourcefulness, leading change, self-navigated learning, understanding self, other people and cultures, technical, scientific and numerical literacy and problem solving and critical thinking. (2024)

Amala works with the MTC to create digital competency–based portfolios for students.

By offering an education to refugees and by focussing on a competency-based approach without the traditional straitjacket of narrow, high-stakes assessments, Amala is broadening access to education both socially and academically.

5   Challenges and Opportunities

Alternative high-school models add reality to the dream of a more inclusive assessment system for students. Many of the examples listed here involve bold entrepreneurial thinking, the forging of new partnerships, and, sometimes, the challenge of leading a vision in a landscape where the vast majority of education providers are locked in the old ways of doing things.

As creative and alternative programmes proliferate, pressure on higher education and employers to recognise these models will increase. Mainstream examination boards will notice the competition, leading them to adapt their models to suit what must and hopefully will become a new normal.

Note

1   UCAS (the University and Colleges Admissions Service) publishes an equivalency table which describes the scores students need to achieve on recognised high-school assessments to be eligible for university entrance in the UK.

References

Amala. (2024). *What is Amala?* https://www.amalaeducation.org/what-is-amala

Detroja, P., Mehta, N., & Agashe, A. (2017). *Swipe to unlock: The primer on technology and business strategy.* Belle Applications, Inc.

GCE [Global Citizenship Diploma]. (n.d.). *About GCD.* https://globalcitizendiploma.org/

Herodotus. (2003). *The histories* (rev'd. ed.; 1st ed., 1954; earlier rev. eds., 1972, 1996). Edited by J. Marincola; translated by A. de Sélincourt. Penguin Classics.

Hess, F. (2023, July 11). What are microcredentials and why should you care? *Forbes*. https://www.forbes.com/sites/frederickhess/2023/07/11/what-are-microcredentials-and-why-should-you-care/

HoloTracker. (2023). Website. https://holotracker.org/

MTC [Mastery Transcript Consortium]. (2021). *What we do*. https://mastery.org/what-we-do/mastery-transcript-and-mtc-learning-record/

SWI [Swiss Information]. (2024). *Apprenticeships in Switzerland*. https://www.swissinfo.ch/eng/politics/apprenticeship-system/43796482

UWCA [United World College of the Atlantic]. (n.d.). *Systems transformation pathway*. https://www.uwcatlantic.org/changemaker-initiatives/systems-transformation-pathway

CHAPTER 9

Higher-Education Efforts at Broadening Assessment

It is not only schools that have recognised the need to broaden assessment: as fast-moving change disrupts social dynamics such as the world of work and migration, it is increasingly and widely understood that the skills, types of knowledge, and dispositions needed to thrive in the world go beyond the remit of academic test–taking. Many universities and colleges are farsighted in their appreciation of this and have adapted their courses and admissions protocols accordingly. Others less so.

1 College Board

Created in Columbia University in the late 1800s and initially known as the "College Entrance Examination Board", the College Board creates multiple tests and programmes for the purpose of entrance criteria into US universities. The College Board runs two major examination centres for the United States: SATs (university admissions tests) and the Advanced Placement (AP) (a rigorous end-of-high-school examination).

It goes without saying that, like most examination boards, the College Board holds enormous sway in determining what kind of assessment students have to take in order to advance to higher education. Any reform instituted by the College Board will have a significant impact on the daily lives of millions of high-school students across the globe.

Numerous criticisms of the College Board's various offers have been lodged over time. These date back to the early 1920s, when marking reliability was put into question,[1] through to more recent complaints about the company's monopolisation of the higher-education admissions landscape. The National Center for Fair & Open Testing has pointed out that an overreliance on narrow admissions testing favours certain demographic groups (FairTest, 2024). Furthermore, SATs and APS come at a cost for test takers, although the government subsidises the latter in state schools.

A significant marking error in 2006 led thousands of students to receive lower scores than they should have gained on their SATs. Marking errors are a staple danger facing examination boards running large-scale assessments. However, the real problem in this case was that the error was known about in December but the College Board didn't respond until March — by that time, a number of university offers had already been made based on those scores. This episode dented the College Board's credibility (Arenson, 2006).

Since the Covid pandemic, when a number of US universities went "test optional" — meaning that they no longer required the SAT for admissions — the AP examination has become more and more popular. The AP examinations have now expanded across all schools in the United States (College Board, 2024), including those in lower–income bracket neighbourhoods.[2]

The AP is seen as a particularly rigorous academic examination that does not fit into the category of those end-of-year projects seeking to broaden assessment; it is part of an endeavour to give access to high-quality education to those who usually cannot afford it. However, "quality" in this case is understood in a traditional conservative sense, essentially equating academic difficulty. In a fairly scathing account, *New York Times* education journalist Dana Goldstein (2023) states that while the effort to expand the AP to low-income students has laudable intentions, roughly 60% of such students taking AP exams in 2023 scored too low for college credit. Furthermore,

> AP curriculums, which are given to schools for free, can be enriching and valuable. But the grueling, multi-hour tests put many low-income students at a disadvantage. Their families have fewer resources to spend on test prep; they may not speak English as a first language; and they may have attended elementary and middle schools that provided less effective preparation. (Goldstein, 2023)

Without reforming the AP so that it escapes the treadmill of academic exercises predicated on social advantage, its expansion will signify not only the propagation of narrow assessments but also the potential exacerbation of the so-called Matthew Effect in education (the rich get richer and the poor get poorer)

The AP has made some efforts to diversify the courses it offers, including courses on race and indigeneity and on the nature of assessment. A 2023 AP conference laid out plans to include student projects in the final assessments. The senior vice president of the AP, Trevor Packer, also noted that project-based assessments were more popular with students (Johnson, 2023).

2   Test-Optional Pathways

Earlier in this book we looked at the manner in which many examination boards generated results during the Covid-19 crisis and subsequent cancellation of examinations. This was primarily through algorithmic calculations of scores using predictions and historical data on the accuracy of schools' student-achievement predictions. How did universities respond to the effect that the pandemic had on admissions testing?

Since Covid-19 disrupted the dynamics of SAT testing quite severely, universities went "test optional". Effectively, this meant that they no longer required SATs and admitted students based on other sources of information concerning their academics and social engagement.

However, the movement to drop SATs predated Covid-19. In 2001 Richard Atkinson, the president of the University of California,

> recommended that colleges stop using the SAT and switch to tests tied more closely to the high school curriculum. Between 2001 and 2005, studies conducted in California confirmed that high school grades are the best indicator of college performance, and this correlation becomes stronger as students progress toward graduation. (DePaul University, 2021)

The University of California's decision was based on questions of assessment validity and fairness (with particular regard to social justice) more than anything else. FairTest's director Harry Feder stated,

> [A]dmissions offices increasingly recognize that test requirements, given their negative disparate impact on Black and Latinx applicants, are "race-conscious" factors, which can create unfair barriers to access higher education [and] that standardized exams are, at best, weak predictors of academic success and largely unrelated to college-ready skills and knowledge. (FairTest, 2023)

In 2004, Bates College ran a detailed longitudinal study comparing the university performances of admissions test takers and with that of non–admissions test takers only to find that there was no significant difference between the two groups. In fact, non–test takers actually had very slightly higher college graduation rates (DePaul University, 2011).

So the movement to go test-optional is an effort to escape the checkerboard of high-stakes, narrow assessments and to look for more valid and fair alternatives. By allowing students to apply based on their grade averages and personal statements, these universities are opening a pathway that is less stressful and more rounded. During the Covid test-optional spate across US universities, all eight Ivy League colleges turned away from ACTs and SATs.

However, after Covid-19, whereas many universities remained test-optional, others started to question the validity of this approach, claiming that standardised testing actually mitigates ethnic and socioeconomic bias. Thus, Yale, MIT, and Dartmouth declared in 2024 that they would return to admissions testing.

> Yale cited internal findings that the current policy can disadvantage first-generation, low income, and rural students, and announced it would adopt a "test flexible" regime under which applicants will be required to submit scores from the SAT or ACT, or else release all their AP or IB test scores. (Komatsu, 2024)

On its website, Yale justifies this decision as follows:

> A student's transcript tells the selection committee much about a candidate's preparation: it provides evidence of a student's academic drive, resourcefulness, and performance over time. Testing can fill in additional parts of the picture. Tests can highlight an applicant's areas of academic strength, reinforce high school grades, fill in gaps in a transcript stemming from extenuating circumstances, and — most importantly — identify students whose performance stands out in their high school context. (Yale University, 2024)

The argument, fundamentally, was that non-test options are more open to subjectivity and bias, precisely because the student's personality comes through much more strongly and this often leads to recruitment bias. For this reason, those who admit students unconsciously choose people who look and sound as they do.

However, from the perspective of broadening assessment in the name of inclusion, this feels like a step backward. Much research has shown that success in highly academic programmes and admissions tests correlates positively with social advantages (Steiner et al., 2024.; Struhl & Vargas, 2012). This is particularly the case for SATs and ACTs. In fact, both systems (test-optional and admission testing) reveal unfairness in different ways.

SATs test "language, punctuation, and grammar skills necessary for success in college" (White, 2024) but are fairly far in utility from the type of language used in day-to-day work and life interactions. This is not to say that the study of the more arcane intricacies of punctuation and grammar is not necessary for certain academic pathways, but to insist on them as standard entry requirements for a variety of different university courses seems excessively traditionalist.

Former university guidance counsellor and *Forbes* contributor Scott White points out:

> The mathematics sections of these tests test skills that an extremely small slice of the population needs or uses. The skills being tested, arithmetic, algebra, geometry, and trigonometry, are the same and have been in place for over a century despite the drastic changes in who goes to college and what is being demanded by our workforce. Not a single common career skill[3] mentioned by almost any major publication is tested by the math section of the SAT/ACT. (White, 2024)

The danger of Ivy League and top-tier universities reverting to standardised admissions testing is that they set the tone for others to follow. This could lead to a wider retrogressive movement, plunging students further into the world of high-stakes testing rather than freeing them from it.

3   Interviews

Some universities interview students as part of admissions testing. Why don't most do this? And is interviewing a broadening or a narrowing of the assessment process?

First, it's important to realise that the assessment purpose of interviews is not the same for all universities. At the time of writing, out of the eight Ivy League schools, for example, only Brown asks for a video portfolio; Yale recommends an interview for evaluative purposes, and the other six use interviews *after* the admissions decision, for informative purposes (Safier, 2024). In the UK, Oxford and Cambridge are well known for their interview process but are not the only universities that make a final decision based on this.

In general, the purpose of the interview is to assess the candidate's personality and to evaluate their thinking processes and values. It could be argued that this allows for an appreciation of the students that is at once broader — since interviews can go in many directions and allow students the agency to respond however they wish — and more personal. In general, interviews are more authentic assessments than written assignments, and they mirror real-life and workplace tasks (like job interviews and interactions in professional meetings) much more closely than test taking does. Furthermore, the skill of on-your-feet thinking, which is evaluated in interviews, is a clear indicator of a certain type of intellectual vivacity that cannot be masked by tutor-enhanced test-taking preparation.

History student and journalist Kieran Dodds, in a personal reflection published in *The Guardian,* said that

> interviews are more efficient, and indeed fairer, than the cold, artificial and misleading personal statement. They help determine which students, regardless of background, will flourish at the university in question. They mirror job interviews which all students will face later in life. Most of all, they represent an opportunity — especially for state-school applicants. (Dodds, 2012)

Most universities do not run interviews for logistical and financial purposes since the people power needed to administer such an undertaking is colossal, especially when one considers the increasing mass of undergraduate university applications. Furthermore, one might make an argument against interviews in the name of assessment reliability, as the variation in subjective judgement from one interviewer to the next will be considerable.

4   Personal Statements

As part of their admission process, many universities require the student to submit a personal statement, to give the admissions team an idea of their profile. In theory, this should be a positive step in the direction of broadening assessment because it allows students to showcase strengths and passions that a grade transcript might not capture. However, these statements can be highly proctored and relay social advantage. In a 2010 UK Sutton Trust report on personal statements, it was pointed out that "private school students not only tend to submit more carefully-crafted statements but generally have a more privileged set of experiences about which to boast such as work experience at blue chip employers" (Walker, 2012).

Over time, personal statements have become like mini-CVs listing all the sports, extracurricular activities, social impact and leadership work a student has done. From a "broadening assessment" perspective, this is a good thing because it implies the reward of a broad range of skills. However, it can quickly become a race to the top of student activity, putting pressure on students to outperform their peers and produce *ubermensch*-type statements that many working adults would struggle to compete with. The backwash of this form of assessment is that it is unregulated and sets no boundaries on what should reasonably be expected of a young person making their way into early adulthood.

5   Sports and Arts Scholarships

In the quest to widen admissions criteria for entry to higher education, it is not only students who are academically gifted who are eligible for bursaries. Those who are gifted in sports and arts can also gain entry to colleges and universities through fast-tracking and bursaries. At face value, this is a positive step in the direction of inclusion and a holistic appreciation of learning.

There is a tradition in the United States, in particular, to award athletics scholarships to students with strong track records, and who show promise, in certain sports. Scouts and coaches attend athletics meetings to decide which students they will bring onto the university team and, in doing so, offer tuition.

The infamous "Varsity Blues" scandal in 2019 saw this system being abused by wealthy parents who would bribe coaches and even admissions officers to accept students into programmes through the sports door despite, in some cases, their not actually being athletes.

Creative arts and design scholarships also exist across several universities, allowing students gifted in those areas access to higher-education opportunities. Admissions criteria tend to be based on portfolios, as is the general tradition of assessment in the fine arts. (The assessment of music education, on the other hand, tends to be very much performance-driven.) It could be argued that portfolio assessment is a viable alternative to examination-based evaluation since students have time to compile their work and the portfolio demonstrates the process of learning as much as the final product — something that is more valid as a construct. Indeed, a number of alternative assessment systems involve portfolio work.

6   Assessment Constructs

At the centre of the debate around the type of assessment used for university admissions is the construct of fairness: whether a purely meritocratic, academic, admission test–related, interview-based, portfolio-based, or even more general evaluation is a stronger indicator for potential admissions — and to what extent some form of adjustment or derogation should be considered to make the results more equitable (Boliver & Powell, 2023).

Admissions protocols change through time. Universities move through cycles of more or less traditional or experimental methods to determine access, whereas many state universities in Europe, for example, simply require students to pass the national matriculation for automatic acceptance (although often undergraduate attrition rates in these environments are high).

The North American university system tends to be more holistic in its appreciation of student gifts and talents. It models the type of broadness that, if embraced by more universities, might allow for more diverse talent recognition, freeing students from the checkerboard of Carnegie-unit academics and their corresponding narrow assessments. Increasingly, universities in other countries — in particular, IE University in Spain and Science Po in France — are embracing a more holistic assessment design. However, most British, Swiss, Indian, Chinese, and state universities in Europe remain tightly focussed on grades and grades only.

Notes

1   Which is not surprising for an examination board running large-scale assessments — an operation which is far from error-free.
2   Meaning schools whose students primarily come from families in lower income brackets.
3   Decision-making, multitasking, creative problem-solving, collaboration, communication, professionalism, integrity, management, initiative, empathy, leadership, and teamwork.

References

Arenson, K. W. (2006, March 23). SAT problems even larger than reported. *New York Times*. https://www.nytimes.com/2006/03/23/education/sat-problems-even-larger-than-reported.html

Boliver, V., & Powell, M. (2023). Competing conceptions of fair admission and their implications for supporting students to fulfil their potential at university. *Perspectives, 27*(1), 8–15. https://doi.org/10.1080/13603108.2022.2063429

College Board. (2024). AP program reports. *Reports*. https://reports.collegeboard.org/ap-program-results

DePaul University. (2011). *A brief history of the test optional movement in higher education*. https://offices.depaul.edu/enrollment-management/test-optional/Documents/HistoryOfTOinHigherEd_EMatters3-18-11.pdf

Dodds, K. (2012, December 12). Are university interviews a fair way to pick students? *The Guardian*. https://www.theguardian.com/education/2012/dec/12/are-university-interviews-fair

FairTest. (2023, June 7). *Vast majority of U.S. colleges and universities extend SAT/ACT optional admission policies to Fall 2024 and beyond*. https://fairtest.org/vast-majority-of-u-s-colleges-and-universities-extend-act-sat-optional-policies-to-fall-2024-applicants-or-beyond/

FairTest. (2024). *Test optional and test free colleges*. https://fairtest.org/test-optional-list/

Goldstein, D. (2023, November 18). Why is the College Board pushing to expand Advanced Placement? *New York Times.* https://www.nytimes.com/2023/11/18/us/college-board-ap-exams-courses.html

Johnson, E. (2023, August 10). *What's ahead for the AP program: Discussing and prioritizing potential changes.* AP Annual Conference. https://allaccess.collegeboard.org/whats-ahead-ap-program-discussing-and-prioritizing-potential-changes

Komatsu, S. (2024, February 29). Testing the waters on test-optional admissions. *Harvard Crimson.* https://www.thecrimson.com/article/2024/2/29/editorial-yale-required-testing/

Safier, R. (2024). SAT / ACT prep online guides and tips: The complete list of colleges that require interviews. *PrepScholar.* https://blog.prepscholar.com/full-list-of-colleges-that-require-interviews

Steiner, E. D., Morales, S., & Mulhern, C. (2024). *Access to mathematics learning and postsecondary preparation opportunities in high school: Findings from the 2023 American Mathematics Educator Study.* RAND Corporation. https://www.rand.org/pubs/research_reports/RRA2836-3.html

Struhl, B., & Vargas, J. (2012). *Taking college courses in high school: A strategy guide for college readiness—The college outcomes of dual enrollment in Texas.* https://eric.ed.gov/?id=ED537253

Walker, P. (2010, December 7). State school pupils face unfair fight for university places, charity warns. *The Guardian.* https://www.theguardian.com/education/2012/dec/07/state-school-pupils-unfair-fight-university-places

White, S. (2024, March 18). The SAT: The tail wagging the dog. *Forbes.* https://www.forbes.com/sites/scottwhite/2024/03/18/the-satthe-tail-wagging-the-dog/

Yale University. (2024). *Standardized testing requirements & policies.* https://admissions.yale.edu/standardized-testing

CHAPTER 10

Assessment of Talent in the Workplace

In searching for assessment paradigms that look to shift the focus from narrow, high-stakes academic testing to a broader appreciation of human potential, high schools have much to learn from the world of work. In an analysis of necessary competences for work in the 21st century, certain assessment tools and approaches to professional growth provide valuable keys to unlocking the doors that remain closed to many diverse human gifts in schools.

Although many workplaces still operate in a traditional fashion — with inflexible approaches to job descriptions, recruitment, and evaluation pegged to such constructs as qualifications, experience, and technical skills — more-forward-looking institutions make it clear that what they are looking for in employees is more subtle than what a curriculum vitae describes. These institutions look to the intangible but ultimately more important dimensions of mindset, interpersonal aptitude, and creativity.

Each year the World Economic Forum (WEF) publishes a set of skills that thought leaders from the world of work believe are the most essential. These change slightly from year to year but in recent years have tended to involve critical thinking, creativity, problem solving, systems thinking, teamwork, and skills related to the analysis of big data.

A 2023 WEF report on the future of jobs reported that roughly "23% of jobs are expected to change by 2027, with 69 million new jobs created and 83 million eliminated" (WEF, 2024). Areas for growth in the job market included green transitioning and the consequent localisation of supply chains. The predicted fastest-growing jobs were "AI and machine learning specialists, sustainability specialists, business intelligence analysts and information security specialists; largest absolute growth is expected in education, agriculture and digital commerce" (WEF, 2024). The World Bank predicts that "megatrends such as automation, action against climate change, the digitalization of products and services, and a shrinking and aging labor force, will transform over 1.1 billion jobs in the next decade" (World Bank, 2024); whereas, "[a]bout 450 million youth (7 out of 10) are economically disengaged, due to lack of adequate skills to succeed in the labor market" (World Bank, 2024).

The rise of artificial intelligence, particularly Generative Artificial Intelligence (GenAI) has and will have an important impact on the nature of work and education. According to *Forbes* contributor and leadership professor Eli Amdur, GenAI has made 17 skills and/or types of knowledge necessary to

© UNESCO IBE, 2025 | DOI:10.1163/9789004714205_010

expand upon in order to prepare for the future of work in that sector: programming languages; AI frameworks and libraries; neural networks and deep learning; machine learning; mathematics; data manipulation and analysis; natural language processing (NLP); computer vision; reinforcement learning; version control; cloud computing; model evaluation and hyperparameter tuning; deployment and scaling; AI ethics and bias; collaboration and communication; ongoing learning; problem solving and creativity (Amdur, 2023).

Apart from mathematics, few if any of these skills are assessed explicitly or intentionally in traditional high-school examinations unless it is in computer science or related specialised areas chosen by students.

This is merely one example of the mismatch between the skills required to flourish in the world of school assessments with those required to flourish in the world of work. Although the area of GenAI is a particularly salient example because of how it is growing as an industry, this mismatch can be seen in other areas of work, such as medicine, the arts, and finances. At a broader level, most if not all professions are being and most likely will continue to be disrupted heavily by the rise of powerful technologies. This means that the skills, knowledge, and attitudes needed in the world of work have evolved — and this should be reflected in the type of assessments students experience at school and at university.

If most school curricula do not reflect the skills, knowledge, and dispositions related to this fast-changing landscape, then a number of workplace practices and evaluation systems enhance and nurture them and can serve as models for schools.

1   Personality Tests

The work of psychologists during the last century, in particular the theories of Carl Gustav Jung, has shaped the way that the human psyché is appreciated in relation to the workplace. Jung's pioneering work on personality led to the development of such matrices as the Myers-Briggs type indicator, the CAPP test, and the DISC.

These tests assess answers to situational questions so as to indicate test takers' behavioural preferences, values, and beliefs.

For Jung, a set number of personality styles could predict, to a certain extent, individual and group behaviours and choices. A well-known one is the introvert/extrovert binary; each of us has elements of both within us, but one tendency tends to dominate the other. The more aware we become of this, the better we understand ourselves and, perhaps more importantly, the more likely we are to be able to change some dimension of our personality. That is, such metacognitive self-awareness pushes us to shape our behaviours toward a personality type that may not come naturally to us.

These psychological assessments are used in several professional processes such as recruitment and personal development because they are directly related to competences necessary in the workplace: teamwork, communication, interaction with others, listening skills, leadership, resilience, and empathy. Indeed, if these were assessed in school, the graduation profile of students would be very different to the scholarly one in force today. Industrial psychology describes highly relevant life skills; related personality tests assess dispositions and attitudes rather than declarative knowledge and procedural skills. Since it is impossible to study for these tests, were they to be used at the end of high school to make student competences visible, the stress and burden of test preparation would be mitigated, allowing for a more serene pace to the curriculum with a focus on learning rather than test preparation.

Schools can learn a lot from these types of assessment due to their construct validity: they measure transferable and practical, applicable skills. Furthermore, they are low stakes in their design since it is nearly impossible to cheat on a personality test. Questions need to be answered relatively quickly; further, they are jumbled in a way that makes it difficult to play the system and offer untruthful answers well enough to give a convincing "score" (scores reflect personality types). Lastly, personality tests involve introspection, the development of intrapersonal skills, and self-reflection. Self-awareness is a particularly valuable dimension of learning and breaks away from the tradition of exogenous testing, which is focused on output and performance as opposed to self-knowledge and self-realisation — both important traits in professional fields.

Jung believed that there were four fundamental aspects to personality: thinking, feeling, sensation, and intuition (SAP, 2024). People's tendencies, captured in their answers to the questions in a personality test, tend to situate them on an axis between these personality types. Jungian analysis sees the psyche as both conscious and unconscious, drawing from collective and individual phenomena to form a state of being. When students understand where they fall on this axis of personality types, they will be able to reflect more intentionally on their predilections and assumptions at unconscious as well as conscious levels.

The use of personality tests for psychological diagnoses and job entry has been heavily criticised both when interpretation is too rigid (pigeonholing people into personality types) and for many issues concerning their scientific validity (Murphy Paul, 2004). Despite this, their potential for service in schools is considerable and has not been explored beyond limited uses such as university guidance counselling.

Were schools to explore student potential using personality tests or, in any case, evaluations in the spirit of personality tests, it would allow students to use this information to make informed decisions and develop personal goals, appreciating a wider ambit of their potential than traditionally narrow testing regimes reflect.

2 Growth and Evaluation: Different Approaches

Performance evaluation is a core part of the human resources of any organisation. There are different approaches to how this can be done and, here again, schools can learn from practice in the field.

Traditional models tend to be top down, based on observation and evaluation. Employees work to a job description; various project objectives, and sometimes evaluation, are analysed according to an assessment grid. This system of job-performance measurement is not entirely unlike a traditional grading system in that it is built on compliance and numerical scoring against set standards.

A method used in coaching (once more drawing from Jungian theories) is based less on compliance and evaluation and much more on personal growth in the light of personally conceived goals. The growth model involves 1:1 supervisor-to-supervisee discussions founded on what is important to the supervisee, how they/she/he wishes to develop, and which goals have been set to get there — precisely by the supervisee's thinking through their goals rather than the supervisor's imposing them.

The core idea in this approach is that each employee has the keys to unlock problems and barriers before them; that with some reflection on the inner resources available, and through scaffolded Socratic questioning, the employee can find solutions. By giving agency to the person being coached (the supervisee), the chances of the goals being more authentic are greater.

The tenets of this approach come from positive psychology (Seligman & Csikszentmihalyi, 2014; Gibbon, 2020). This field of psychology is based on well-being and the relationship the mind has with decision making and emotions. Positive psychology explores the potential people have to ideate thoughts that determine subsequent impressions of what is possible. The field also allows for considerable metacognitive reflection, equipping those who use it with the tools to reflect on the values that motivate their actions and concrete goals they might wish to attain.

Despite some consolidated understanding of the virtues of positive psychology in schools and some efforts to introduce it, it remains a fringe activity, not having gained the traction that other innovations and reforms have (White, 2016). This is to do with cost, understanding, and variability of available models. Closely related to positive psychology is life coaching, used most frequently in personal spheres of self-actualisation, career planning, and personal wellbeing. Here, again, are some particularly powerful ideas that should be considered in the new assessment paradigms schools need, especially at the end of high school when students are planning their next moves, thinking about the future and, eventually, their future careers.

The practice of life coaching is contested and, in some cases, the use of the term "life coaching" can be misleading and even abusive, involving spin doctors, salespeople, and underqualified, unregulated self-made entrepreneurs (Bishop, 2024). However, when done well and when regulated, by companies such as the International Coaching Federation (ICF, 2024), it is an effective method of self-assessing and goal setting.

The closest that present-day end-of-high-school assessments get to this paradigm is the personal statement, used by British and US universities, whereby a student will articulate their story, passions, and goals. However, it is commonly accepted that university admissions officers, at least in some countries, have little if any time to look at these carefully (Adams, 2023).

A new assessment model should allow for this component of self-reflection (which, in the very process of its development, becomes a powerful learning experience) and should design it to ensure that the person assessing it can fully appreciate the information. There are ways of doing this using frameworks, high-level syntheses of student learning journeys, and technology to curate the information (see the final chapter of this book).

By separating evaluation from growth and by focussing much more on the latter, assessment systems allow for more personal flourishing and richer information on learning.

3   Replacing Performance Reviews with Ongoing Feedback:
       Implications for Learning and the World of Work

Performance reviews are thoroughly embedded in the psychology of industrialisation. Some of the earliest known instances of evaluating end-of-year performance go back to the 19th-century textile industry (which was driven by the slave trade) (Samuel, 2013). Managers were judged against the productivity of their annual output: the rewards would be compensatory, and the consequences for poor productivity would ultimately be termination. This system of rewarding based on a crude output model pushed greater "productivity", which ultimately meant harsher exploitation.

This scientific-management approach was further developed in the army. During WWI, there was a need to establish some sort of ranking or evaluation system to decide who should be discharged from service due to inadequate performance according to a merit system (Cappelli & Tavis, 2016). As many elements of capitalism, industrial psychology, and social planning developed quickly after WWII, so did performance management — entering the domains of business, social services, and industry — particularly for people with extra responsibilities, managers, and leaders.

And as is so often the case in education, there was a mirroring effect in schools and universities of these broader sociological developments. Foucault has shown — in books like *Discipline and Punish* (1975) and *Madness and Civilisation* (1961) — that schools, hospitals, and prisons were built according to normative principles of power, behavioural codification, and control. Although he did not elaborate the point fully concerning assessment per se, the end-of-high-school, high-stakes summative assessment model clearly echoes the industrial approach to performance: a year's (or more) work is evaluated and the results determine future pathways (failure, passing, accelerated future opportunity). So, a Foucauldian analysis of the structure of the end-of-high-school assessment allows us to draw parallels with traditional performance management in the workplace.

There are three fundamental problems with this approach to performance:

The first is the notion of performance itself, a term steeped in the assumptions of industrial production, output, yield, and capital. Human beings are not conveyor belts in factories, banks, or storing systems. Thus, to calibrate their development against such quantitative metrics, which is essentially treating them like machines, reduces who they are. An employee is more than the KPIs designed to measure performance; a student is more than performance on examinations.

The second problem: a type of "learning bulimia" results when industrial-yield models, based on annual (or quarterly) balance sheets, are transferred to learning; high-stakes summative assessment lends itself to rote learning and a concentrated burst of output, leading to students' forgetting much of what they learned for examinations. One criticism of annual work-performance reviews is that they are essentially backward-looking, requiring employees to think ahead but based on earlier rather than current performance — much as examinations test knowledge learnt in the past. The deeper goal should be to predict, if not prepare for, future learning.

Finally, summative evaluation systems drive metric-related performance behaviour (as opposed to more-authentic learning behaviours). Teachers teach to the test, students learn for grades, employees work toward reports and yardsticks. As the old adage goes, "We measure what we value and we value what we measure". But what exactly is it we are measuring at the end of a year, and how valid could such a measurement really be? In fact, the worry is greatest in the workplace, where such a system could very well push employees to focus on the metric (financial results, for example) to the point where the end justifies the means. Behaviours to arrive at certain goals become problematic, if not abusive and unethical. Systems that are excessively high stakes promote cheating and gaming the system

Many organisations are turning away from the traditional annual performance review to ongoing feedback with a formative purpose. Likewise, assessments in high school should mirror gradual progress alongside, if not instead of, summative assessments. In this way the assessment system promotes learning more and judges it less; it becomes more of a narrative of a learning journey. In order to improve, we need feedback on the fly — what Dylan Wiliam calls "embedded formative assessment" (Wiliam, 2017).

By continually contributing to the portrait of the graduate or the employee, step by step, educational and work institutions will ensure that the learning is richer, the organisational culture more pedagogic, and the final goal more authentic.

References

Adams, R. (2023, June 15). UK university staff only read students' personal statements for two minutes. *The Guardian.* https://www.theguardian.com/education/2023/jun/15/uk-university-staff-only-read-students-personal-statements-for-two-minutes

Amdur, E. (2023, August 19). 17 critical skills for the AI "techie". *Forbes.* https://www.forbes.com/sites/eliamdur/2023/08/19/17-critical-skills-for-the-ai-techie/

Bishop, K. (2024, February 7). The seedy underbelly of the life coaching industry. *BBC Worklife.* https://www.bbc.com/worklife/article/20240206-life-coaching-industry-scams

Cappelli, P., & Tavis, A. (2016). The performance management revolution. *Harvard Business Review.* https://hbr.org/2016/10/the-performance-management-revolution

Gibbon, P. (2020). Martin Seligman and the rise of positive psychology. *Humanities, 41*(3). https://www.neh.gov/article/martin-seligman-and-rise-positive-psychology

ICF [International Coaching Federation]. (2024). *Empowering the world through coaching*. https://coachingfederation.org/

Murphy Paul, A. (2004). *The cult of personality: How personality tests are leading us to miseducate our children, mismanage our companies, and misunderstand ourselves.* Free Press.

Samuel, B. (2013). The origin, concept and value of performance appraisal. *International Journal of Economics, Commerce and Management, 1*(2).

SAP [Society for Analytical Psychology]. (2024). *Jung's model of the psyche.* https://www.thesap.org.uk/articles-on-jungian-psychology-2/carl-gustav-jung/jungs-model-psyche/

Seligman, M. E. P., & Csikszentmihalyi, M. (2014). Positive psychology: An introduction. In *Flow and the foundations of positive psychology: The collected works of Mihaly Csikszentmihalyi.* Springer. https://doi.org/10.1007/978-94-017-9088-8_18

WEF [World Economic Forum]. (2024). *Future of jobs report 2023: Up to a quarter of jobs expected to change in next five years.* https://www.weforum.org/press/2023/04/future-of-jobs-report-2023-up-to-a-quarter-of-jobs-expected-to-change-in-next-five-years/

White, M. A. (2016). Why won't it stick? Positive psychology and positive education. *Psychology of Well-Being, 6*(2). https://doi.org/10.1186/s13612-016-0039-1

Wiliam, D. (2017). *Embedded formative assessment: Strategies for classroom assessment that drives student engagement and learning (The new art and science of teaching).* 2nd ed. Solution Tree Press.

World Bank. (2024). *Skills and workforce development.* https://www.worldbank.org/en/topic/skillsdevelopment

CHAPTER 11

Competences

If assessment should broaden what it currently covers to move beyond academic test–taking ability, what exactly should it be looking to? There is no simple answer to this question as there are many alternative frameworks in circulation. Examples include: the 4D Competencies Framework, developed by the Centre for Curriculum Redesign, which looks at knowledge, skills, character, and meta-learning (Centre for Curriculum Design, 2024); the OECD's 2030 Learning Compass, which explores "core foundations, knowledge, skills, attitudes and values, transformative competencies and a cycle of anticipation, action, and reflection" (OECD, 2024); the Common Ground Collaborative, which focusses on conceptual understanding, competency, and character (Common Ground Collaborative, 2024); the World Economic Forum's Education 4.0 learning taxonomy, which explores skills, attitudes, and values necessary for flourishing in the 21st century (WEF, 2023). Furthermore, many national curriculum schemes, such as those in Singapore (SIT, 2023) and New Zealand (Education Review Office, 2019), develop more than mere academic skills, turning to life skills and attitudes.

What these various taxonomies and frameworks have in common is that they look beyond knowledge alone into skills and attitudes. This is because the nature of knowledge in today's world is much more fluid and transitional than it ever has been in history. To give an example, approaches to science and philosophy throughout the Middle Ages in Europe, largely Ptolemaic and Aristotelian in nature, did not change substantially for roughly a thousand years. However, the body of research and knowledge in several disciplines today — in particular, such areas as neurobiology, epidemiology, immigration studies, and computing — changes every few months. Even history, that seemingly immutable construct, changes rapidly with more in-depth technological and analytical probes into the past and new conjectures over questions concerning the palaeolithic period and ancient history. Theories about Cromagnon and Homo sapiens are updated as technology allows carbon testing to reach further and further back, drawing more evidence into the picture.

What this means is that while core declarative knowledge of transferable epistemes (such as philosophical theories and scientific concepts) remains necessary to learn in school, along with foundational skills such as numeracy and literacy, the ability to store encyclopaedic volumes of knowledge in one's long-term memory is less valorised. What becomes equally, if not more important, is the ability to update that knowledge quickly, to deploy that information in new contexts. As Alvin Toffler famously said: "[T]he illiterate of the twenty-first century will not be those who cannot read and write, but those who cannot learn, unlearn, and relearn" (Amdur, 2022).

The skills needed to thrive socially and through increasingly frequent spans of disruption to society and technology need to be articulated clearly for educational reform to be of consequence. However, skills alone are not enough — they must be guided by values that will ensure that the acquisition and distribution of knowledge contributes to life on earth in positive ways and to the mutual benefit of all.

So while certain types of knowledge remain essential to a good education, the clear trajectory of educational assessment is toward skills and values. The ideas involving a 21st-century–skills curriculum, or competence-based learning, have been amplified over the last 30 years to the point where an array of models now exist as potential alternatives.

Two problems with the taxonomies mentioned previously are that each conflates skills, values, and types of knowledge; and often they have redundancies in the modelling of exactly what students are to know. For example, the OECD speaks of attitudes and values (what is the difference?), the 4D curriculum looks at skills and meta-learning (isn't metacognition a skill already?). Another problem is the "listing" effect of juxtaposing knowledge with skills with attitudes, suggesting that they are separate constructs that need to be developed alongside one another in an accumulation — rather than being a single entity. The particular issue with this effect of accumulation is the "crowded garage effect" (Perkins, 2014), whereby curricula suffer from items being added incessantly to the body of what is to be known and what is to do, leaving the syllabus overcrowded.

To establish a strong framework that is lucid and comprehensive, the first step is to clearly define the constituents of knowledge, skills, and attitudes so that one can comprehend their interrelatedness. Secondly, one needs to elaborate a series of constructs (in other words, a defined number of competences) that contains these elements in a fluid continuity of experience and learning. The term "competence" or "competency" relates to such a construct, hence the growing field of competence-based education. The two terms are nuanced in meaning: a competence is specifically focused on an episteme, while competency tends to be broader; but for this publication, I use the two terms interchangeably.

What exactly is a competence? It is a unity of knowledge (information that has been stored and understood), skill (a technical aptitude), and attitude (a mindset). If, for example, someone understands code for computing, you could say that they are knowledgeable. If they know how to write code and transfer elements of it to other technical situations, you could say that they are skilled. However, what would be the final purpose of mastering the code? What would they do with the code? To what ends would the computers be programmed and what would be the social and economic impacts of this decision? This is where attitude comes in, a term one could associate with values and dispositions. A competent person is not just a skilled, experienced, and/or knowledgeable labourer or social partner but a wise, helpful, interpersonally developed, intrapersonally aware, creative, critical, curious, and kind person.

Competences unite the four elements of learning articulated in the 1996 Delors Report (learning to know, learning to do, learning to be, learning to live together) (Delors, 1996).

Therefore, a competence such as lifelong learning incorporates three key elements: one, the knowledge needed to transfer understanding across contexts (languages, historical and geographical understandings, key concepts) and, two, the skill of navigating unknown and unprecedented situations in which learning will be needed to flourish (e.g., picking up new information relatively quickly, integrating new cultural codes and technical approaches according to new developments). The third element involves the attitudes of curiosity, critical thinking, and passion for learning, which are the drivers for the whole enterprise of lifelong learning.

Once these three elements of knowledge, skills, and attitudes have been united, a competence has been established. This is precisely the construct toward which we should be teaching and assessing in the 21st century given the nature of global demographic, environmental, technical, and political changes — and the social, emotional, technical, and knowledge-based approaches needed to accommodate them. The power of a competence is that it comprises these interrelated dimensions within its conceptual framework.

1   UNESCO IBE's Work and Vision of Curriculum and Competences

In 2017, UNESCO's International Bureau of Education (IBE) launched the publication of three seminal studies on curriculum, competences, and teaching and learning. With the support of numerous research centres, curriculum boards, and academic experts, the papers produced a vision for competence-based learning.

The UNESCO IBE definition of a competence is the developmental capacity to interactively mobilize and ethically use information, data, knowledge, skills, values, attitudes, and technology to engage effectively and act across diverse 21st-century contexts to attain individual, collective, and global good (UNESCO IBE, 2017, p. 27).

To this day, the seven global competences developed by UNESCO IBE constitute a strong framework for curriculum development. They are stable, meaning they will not change over time. Each one is comprised of a cluster of micro competences — that is, more transient, context-specific, and modulable skills, attitudes, and types of knowledge:

> *Lifelong learning*: learning how to learn, curiosity, creativity, critical thinking, communication skills, problem solving, reflection, and innovation.
>
> *Self-agency*: initiative, drive/motivation, endurance/grit/resilience, responsibility, entrepreneurship, accountability, self-management, exercising rights and responsibilities, self-value.
>
> *Interactively using diverse tools and resources*: effective and efficient use of resources, responsible consumption, interfacing with tools.
>
> *Interacting with others*: teamwork, collaboration, negotiation, leadership, followership, conflict management, respect for others.
>
> *Interacting with the world*: balancing rights with responsibilities, balancing freedom with respect, balancing power with restraint, being local and global, being environmental custodians, having global awareness.
>
> *Multi-literateness*: reading and writing, numeracy, digital literacy, data literacy, technological literacy, coding, media literacy, financial literacy, cultural literacy, health literacy.
>
> *Transdisciplinarity*: mastery within and across STEM (sciences, technology, engineering, mathematics), the arts, the humanities, the social sciences, religions, languages, and vocations (Hughes, 2024).

By shifting the discourse from a fragmented one that juxtaposes skills, knowledge, and attitudes — by aiming for holistic constructs that seamlessly integrate the necessary dimensions of learning and being for individual, collective, and public goods — educational practices will be more meaningful, relevant to the needs of today's world, integrated, and comprehensive.

2   The Significance of Competences for the Future of Work

By moving to a competence-based assessment model, schools will be sending the message to students that the institution is interested in more than their academic test–taking ability — it is interested, as well, in their whole person, including their values and mindsets. This will also send a message to employers that a high-school graduate is someone who has developed competences in life-worthy areas and, in such a manner, has been prepared for the world of work.

Indeed, UNESCO IBE's seven global competences speak to the world of work since they describe attributes needed in the professional sphere. For example, take the construct of interacting with others, with its micro competence subset of teamwork, collaboration, negotiation, leadership, followership, conflict management, and respect for others. It becomes clear that these are all crucial in the workspace, even more so than a number of technical skills. However, at school level, they tend to be developed tangentially in extracurricular activities (debate club, community service, theatrical productions) without any serious assessment. By intentionally developing these micro competences through the curriculum and assessing them formally, so as to magnify their importance, schools will be preparing young people to enter the workplace equipped with powerful and relevant social competences.

Another example is self-agency, whose micro competences are initiative, drive/motivation, endurance/grit/resilience, responsibility, entrepreneurship, accountability, self-management, exercising rights and responsibilities, self-value. All are necessary for the resilience, confidence, and self-worth one needs to flourish in the professional sphere without being sidetracked or affected adversely by negative interactions and attacks on morale. When young people enter the world of work, they do not realise that they are stepping into much more than a technical sphere. They discover that work's social and political dimensions, personalities and relationships, and power dynamics — and also the necessary self-preservation and psychological resilience to deal with all these — are every bit as important as one's technical skills.

To flourish in that world — which is primarily social — one must develop intrapersonal and interpersonal qualities. Typically, schools do not teach this, at least not explicitly, and the onboarding process in the workplace does not necessarily deal with these questions, either. The result is that often employees find themselves caught up in difficult professional relationships, which can involve bullying and harassment. They may turn to Human Resources or ombudspersons for solutions, but by this time a lot of damage has already been done. If, on the other hand, schools and universities spent more time working on these competences, building up the repertoire of thinking routines, strategies, and behaviours necessary to thrive in potentially hostile work environments, students would be better prepared and more confident to be upstanders. Those who would usually enter the workplace with a power agenda and (intentionally or not) make life difficult for other people would have been better trained upstream to understand what such behaviour looks like and the dangers of it — and therefore would possibly behave more productively and respectfully in the workplace.

These character-building dimensions of social and emotional learning are also necessary in a school climate, where there are increased reports of anxiety and mental health issues. They can help develop strong anti-bullying and inclusion, diversity, equity, and antiracism programmes. Teaching and assessing constructs such as grit and self-management will prepare young people well for the world of work, and, more generally, for the world of social interactions.

The competence of interactively using diverse tools and resources has associated micro competences of impactful and efficient use of resources, responsible consumption, and interfacing with tools. It thus involves themes through which to educate students to use resources efficiently, in a sustainable and eco-friendly manner — attributes essential for sustainable development goals. If sustainable behaviours and actions are not brought purposefully into the curriculum, there is little chance that that curriculum will address work habits and the culture of overproduction that characterises current-day capitalism. How students use resources should be taught and assessed intentionally to this effect. Related to this is the fast-evolving nature of technology and the need to educate for the skill appropriation, energy, and mindset to handle this complexity and growth meaningfully.

In a globalised economy and with new geographies of immigration and growth, the competence of interacting with the world is an essential construct to develop in young minds. This competence enfolds the micro competences of balancing rights with responsibilities, balancing freedom with respect, balancing power with restraint, being local and global, caring about environmental custodianship, and having global awareness. By working toward these, students will be prepared to enter an interconnected workspace where international affiliations, concern about the increasing scarcity of planetary resources, political decision making, and the dynamics of and responsibility to follow international law are at the forefront of human activity and decision making. It has become necessary for everyone, no matter their station in life or the nature of their work, to be conscious of the potential externalities of their actions and the manner in which their daily actions are, indeed, interactions with the world.

The last two global competences (multi-literateness and transdisciplinarity) remain academic in tenor and implications. This is because, while a competency-based education is necessary to shape the future, mastery within and across STEM, the arts, the humanities, the social sciences, religions, languages, and vocations remains important. This core knowledge forms the epistemic substance from which future citizens will act and transfer knowledge into new situations. Discourses on 21st-century skills that emphasise the changing future of work and the importance of skills, need to nonetheless centre on essential knowledge. If curriculum and assessment highlight the transdisciplinary nature of concepts, or discuss transversal themes in different knowledge-based contexts (e.g., the International Baccalaureate's Theory of Knowledge course), students will learn to apply knowledge to new situations and adapt it to different cultural contexts.

One other central realisation concerning the importance of the transmission, acquisition, storing, and redeployment of knowledge is that it is not always for pragmatic, work-related, or socially beneficial reasons. Much knowledge — particularly historical, cultural, artistic, and social — is aesthetic in nature and simply serves to develop the individual's and the group's identity, appreciation of the world, and ability to understand other people, places, and issues. For this reason, curricula should always have a quotient of "knowledge for knowledge's sake". Education is not solely a means to an economic end but in some regards it is an end in itself, and will be used by each individual in unknown ways. Furthermore, shared knowledge of certain sociological, historical, and geographical facts binds people together with a sense of a common experience, as has been the purpose of national education schemes for the past 200 years.

3   Assessing Competences

Now that we have outlined the seven global competences that are foundational for development in a forward-looking curriculum and assessment programme, how exactly should they be assessed? This is not a simple matter, by any means. Classical test theory seeks to assess a construct that is primarily mental (declarative knowledge, for example) and does this by designing a test that allows the test taker to display what they have stored in their mental apparatus. What is produced, sometimes known as a "mental product", is then assessed according to set criteria; the results of that scoring are used to infer what the mental construct is (how much declarative knowledge the student has about a subject). This is fraught with problems of reliability and validity, and works best when the construct in question aligns well with the style of the test. To give an example: if I wanted to test how well a student had learnt the capitals of countries on the African continent, the test would ask the student to enumerate all, or most, African capital cities. Such a test would be fair, valid, and, if taken under conditions where cheating was not possible and the environment was conducive to test taking, also reliable.

However, if the construct was less rigid and more subtle — for example, understanding the concept of gravity in physics — the mental construct sought would be more open-ended: a written description or a verbal account of the concept to illustrate understanding, for instance. In this case, the manner in which the concept was expressed would determine the extent of the test taker's true understanding. The student might understand what gravity is but have problems putting that understanding into clear written or spoken words, especially if the test language was not the student's first language. A better test might be in the form of a mathematical formula or scientific experiment that would allow the student to show understanding, but there would still be significant problems of validity and reliability depending on how well the experiment was set up, the problem formulated, and the assessment criteria derived. The fuzzier the concept, the greater the risk of unreliable and invalid assessment.

If we turn to competences, which are unities of attitude, knowledge, and skills, the endeavour to map these and assess them accurately is even more difficult. The construct in question is context-specific, brought out in a multitude of potential actions and behaviours, and, given that it is developmental, spans much more than a discrete test-taking snapshot in time could ever translate. It is more or less impossible to set up a test in the manner of classical test theory to assess a competence.

Therefore, the assessment of competences needs to follow these three fundamental principles:

Competences should be assessed over a duration of time (at least 6 months) in order to capture their developmental nature.

Competences should be assessed according to a broad range of tasks, accomplishments, and behaviours, and these should be in naturalistic, authentic settings.

Competence assessment should be scaled in such a way that it captures the specific local cultural context that defines the competences and the manner in which they have come into being. Large-scale uniformed assessments will not be able to do this.

The following chapter illustrates how this can be done in a school setting.

References

Amdur, E. (2022, October 4). "The Illiterate of the 21st Century …". *Forbes.* https://www.forbes.com/sites/eliamdur/2022/10/04/the-illiterate-of-the-21st-century/

Centre for Curriculum Redesign. (2024). *4D competencies framework.* https://curriculumredesign.org/framework/

Common Ground Collaborative. (2024). Website.
https://www.commongroundcollaborative.org/

Delors, J. (1996). *Learning: The treasure within.* Highlights of the Report to UNESCO of the International Commission on Education for the Twenty-first Century. UNESCO. https://unesdoc.unesco.org/ark:/48223/pf0000109590

Education Review Office. (2019). *The key competencies: Realising the potential of the New Zealand curriculum.* http://www.ero.govt.nz

Hughes, C. (2024). Reinventing high school transcripts: The learner passport. *International School Parent.* https://www.internationalschoolparent.com/articles/reinventing-high-school-transcripts-the-learner-passport/

OECD [The Organization for Economic Cooperation and Development]. (2024). *2030 Learning Compass.* https://www.oecd.org/en/data/tools/oecd-learning-compass-2030.html

Perkins, D. (2014). *Future wise: Educating our children for a changing world.* John Wiley & Sons.

SIT [Singapore Institute of Technology]. (2023, August 14). *The future of learning: How competency-based education is shaping skills development.* https://www.singaporetech.edu.sg/news/future-learning-how-competency-based-shaping-skills-development

UNESCO IBE [International Bureau of Education]. (2017). *Future competences and the future of curriculum.* UNESCO IBE.

WEF [World Economic Forum]. (2023, January 13). *Defining Education 4.0: A taxonomy for the future of learning.* White paper. https://www.weforum.org/publications/defining-education-4-0-a-taxonomy-for-the-future-of-learning/

CHAPTER 12

The International School of Geneva and UNESCO International Bureau of Education

The International School of Geneva, commonly known as Ecolint, is the world's first international school. With over 4,500 students and 143 student nationalities, it is one of the largest international schools in the world. Founded in 1924, it was also the birthplace of the Model United Nations system in 1953 and the International Baccalaureate Diploma Programme in 1968 (Ecolint, 2024).

The founders of the school worked for the League of Nations, the International Labour Office, and the Rousseau Institute. This last organisation, ensconced in the pedagogies of Freinet, Froebel, Dewey, and Montessori, also led the creation of the International Bureau of Education (IBE), whose director for 40 years was Jean Piaget.

Both of these organisations (Ecolint and UNESCO IBE) have been at the forefront of developments in education over the past 100 years. The two institutions united in 2017 to articulate guiding principles for learning in the 21st century that inform Ecolint's strategy on questions of curriculum and pedagogy. Concerning principles of assessment specifically within that framework, the document states:

> Assessment should use a large variety of sources of evidence to help students with different learning styles achieve mastery of learner outcomes and lifelong learning; should largely be derived from authentic materials that allow students to come into contact with real-life situations; should allow students from a variety of backgrounds to show what they can do and what they know in conditions that are fair and equitable. (Hughes & Acedo, 2017)

These are some of the foundational tenets of assessment that address problems of validity created by excessively high stakes and narrow constructs.

In 2018, the two institutions collaborated on the design of a competence-based curriculum framework called the "Universal Learning Programme" (Hughes, 2020). This framework uses UNESCO IBE's global competences to assess learning in subjects and through projects (Hughes, 2024). While students are engaged in learning experiences in traditional epistemes such as science and humanities, it is not only their academic ability that is nurtured but also several interpersonal, intrapersonal, and real-world constructs (life-long learning, self-agency, interacting with others, interactively using diverse tools and resources, interacting with the world, transdisciplinarity, and multi-literateness). (See Chapter 11 for an expanded discussion of these competences.)

These competences are assessed through different subjects. For example, science educators will look not only at students' skills and types of knowl-edge inherently associated with the subject but also at their data-literacy and problem-solving skills; students studying philosophy will not only explore con-cepts but also be called upon to show accountability for their own ideas and to demonstrate global awareness. Mathematics students are assessed on their initiative as well as their mathematical thinking; while physical education stu-dents are assessed on self-management and leadership as well as on their work directly with physical education. Further, the Universal Learning Programme has students engage in transdisciplinary projects focused on the development of their character, passion, and mastery of their subject.

Since assessment protocols will always be related to the curriculum con-struct, then if more school programmes wove assessments of competences into classroom activities, learning would move closer to the type of relevance needed for a world in which skills, attitudes, and knowledge work in a harmo-nised, fluid way. Embedding competences in the learning outcomes of subjects and school projects, as the Universal Learning Programme does, is an impor-tant step to take.

Further, if assessment is broadened, then it should not only relate to the construct of classroom subjects but to life outside of school, too, for it is here where many competences are developed.

In 2021, Ecolint used the global competences framework to create an alter-native transcript called the "Ecolint Learner Passport" (Hughes, 2023). The purpose of the passport is to capture students' competences in a variety of settings and to explore a more holistic and inclusive manner of assessing gifts and talents.

1   The Ecolint Learner Passport

The passport was designed collaboratively by teachers, students, university guidance counsellors, and leaders at Ecolint, with recurring input from techni-cal experts at UNESCO IBE. After an initial pilot involving 40 students, feed-back loops, and iterative changes to the design of the passport, from 2021 to 2024 it was rolled out for all high-school seniors, then for students in their final two years, and finally for the last four years of high school.

The last four years of high school usually correspond to High School Diploma credit, giving students a grade-point average that is of paramount importance for entry into North American universities. The passport sits alongside this transcript so as to give university admissions officers and employers (and anyone else) information about the student's holistic development. The hope is that a sufficient number of tertiary education and postsecondary institutions will recognise the passport for it to eventually replace the regular high school diploma.

Any potential activity that a student might be involved in is mapped according to the competences that it embodies. For example, if a student is involved in a project dedicated to sustainable development, the global competence "interacting with the world" is evoked; if they earn some form of extra certification or badge, they are attributed with the competence of "lifelong learning"; if involved in collective sports, they are recognised as "interacting with others".

For academics, the passport also recognises the competences evoked in learning. To align subjects with competences, the assessment criteria for each academic subject was mapped against the UNESCO IBE global competences; two competences per subject were evoked as particularly salient in the assessment design. For example, critical thinking, a microcompetence of lifelong learning, features prominently in the assessment criteria of humanities subjects; lifelong learning is therefore one of the global competences evoked for the humanities. For the natural sciences, subject-assessment criteria typically focus on experimental skills; hence, a global competence evoked is "interactively using diverse tools and resources". This is true for any curriculum framework, not specifically or uniquely for the Universal Learning Programme.

If a student has shown outstanding commitment in an extracurricular activity or area of development outside of the formal curriculum, this is reflected in the amount of competence credit they are given within that learning area. Someone who goes above and beyond in their commitment and participation in a school play, for example, will be attributed more of the "interacting with others" competence credit than someone who is also in the play but not as invested.

A conversion table allows academic achievement to be automatically translated into competence attainment. In this manner, the Ecolint Learner Passport recognises the achievements of academic students alongside those of athletes, artists, learners engaged in social impact work, community service, out-of-school projects in entrepreneurship, and a host of other competence-building activities. Students are allowed to shine according to their strengths rather than solely within a rigid and narrow band of criteria. This is particularly powerful for students who are excluded from the realm of high-stakes academic testing because of their profile — examples include neurodivergent students, those who might have difficulties with the language of the curriculum since it is not their own, and students who struggle to perform in the pressurised environment of test taking that characterises examinations.

If more postsecondary institutions generalised and accepted the Ecolint Learner Passport model, students unable to access the physical sites of educational institutions would nonetheless be able to gain recognition for the advancement of their informal learning. Systems and processes recognising learning that takes place outside of institutions have become more necessary than ever. This is partly due to the expansion of online access to information and the inherent possibilities for self-education built into these new types of platforms. It is also due to the fact that over 250 million children worldwide still cannot access formal education — while many of them could, arguably, gain educational recognition through a system like the passport despite not having been formally educated.

A number of universities — mainly North American "top tier" ones, as well as universities in Spain — have recognised the Ecolint Learner Passport. Universities in other parts of the world are yet to do so. It is the hope of the designers that it will gain more traction and recognition through time.

2   The Coalition to Honour All Learning

In 2022, after the launch of the Ecolint Learner Passport, several heads of school met for a series of online discussions on how assessment might be broadened across schools. The group rapidly grew in number and was joined by representatives of curriculum boards and universities. This became the Coalition to Honour All Learning, which at the time of this writing includes members from more than 50 learning institutions.

Below is a statement by the coalition:

> We believe that while academic knowledge has a crucial role in the development of the child, the development of competences is equally important. Competences are more than knowledge: they also represent skills and dispositions. Our schools are all focussed on the development of competences that equip young people not just for academics, but for life.
>
> We see that the vast majority of universities, colleges and post-secondary institutions require students to submit grade transcripts to make them eligible for further studies. While some institutions are prepared to look

beyond this to the whole child, the majority of post-secondary institutions request academic subject grades only.

We contend that this has the effect of narrowing the curriculum to a limited and restrictive experience that forces students and teachers to prioritise academic subject achievement above all else. Hence, as students progress towards the end of schooling, the experience becomes less and less inclusive. Furthermore, the end of Secondary/High School is at odds with our broader curriculum objective of educating the whole child for lifeworthy competences.

This situation puts tremendous stress on students since terminal assessments, in order to meet post-secondary admissions requirements, are both narrow and high-stakes; they exclude those who are gifted in ways that these assessments do not capture.

Therefore, we invite all post-secondary institutions, including universities, colleges and industries across the globe, to open their admissions criteria beyond academic subject grades and to recognise competences as captured in alternative school transcripts. (Coalition, 2024)

In 2024 the Coalition published a united call for education-system reform for universities, employers, and curriculum boards to consider. Over 150 school and educational board leaders signed it, including the directors of the United World Colleges, the International Baccalaureate, the Council of International Schools, and the International School of Geneva. This united call is for systems around the world to design assessment systems that allow students to flourish and showcase their multiple gifts, be they academic or not:

School communities, education organisations, researchers and policymakers are increasingly acknowledging that, while academic knowledge has an important role in the development of the child, so too does the development of competences (knowledge, skills, and dispositions).

Education systems continue to emphasise a narrow definition of student success based on assessments limited to a few academic disciplines. These models are being challenged by radical and fast-paced societal, environmental and technological changes. We must reform education systems to focus on developing individual and collective capacities to support human flourishing. (Coalition, 2024)

2.1   *The Need for Unity of Purpose but Plurality of Models*

The Ecolint Learner Passport is one model out of several to adapt the end-of-high-school assessment to a more inclusive design. However, it has the advantage of offering a cohesive and coherent framework of competences, developed by UNESCO IBE, through which student learning can be curated, celebrated, and enhanced. For this reason, the International School of Geneva has made the Ecolint Learner Passport's criteria and design features open to any user in the world, so that other schools and even students directly might use it to have their learning recognised.

For the Ecolint Learner Passport to have more currency, the number of institutions using it and recognising it has to increase. Against a stage of heavily institutionalised assessment practices with political and financial backing — accrediting agencies, ministries of education, and commercial organisations who fund and endorse them — this is a difficult thing to do since such a reform appears as a threat to existing practices. Further, since current assessment rituals have been in place for several decades, stakeholders look to them as irrefutable and permanent. These structural support systems influence superstructural elements — such as belief that these assessment models are irreplaceable — often carried most actively by parents who went through similar experiences as students and see them as necessary for their own children.

The goal of the Ecolint Learner Passport is for more schools to adopt it, from differently resourced and culturally framed contexts, so that many more learners across the planet might use it. However, at the broadest philosophical level, it is the wish of the Coalition to Honour All Learning to see alternative transcripts — like the Ecolint Learner Passport, but not necessarily *only* the passport or systems identical to the passport — flourish across different systems and contexts.

2.2   *Scale and Culture: Changing the Paradigm of Mass Assessment to a More Localised Model*

For change to be meaningful, the present model of high-school assessment, which is largely uniform across contexts, needs to be disrupted. Massified, large-scale assessments cannot nurture the subtle competences that the passport and similar other alternative assessments are concerned with. In fact, one of the problems with externally assessed examinations is that since many different students, and cultural contexts, are engaging with a construct that is high stakes, assessments err on the side of reliability, not validity, since they must accordingly reduce the subtlety of their task at hand. Cost is another feature to consider: the cheapest assessments are those that can be machine marked, and these tend to assess declarative knowledge given the necessary binary structure of computer-marked answers.

Therefore, accrediting agencies, higher-education institutions, employers, and postsecondary institutions in general need to accept that each learning ecosystem will invariably design slightly different assessments. In this way, the assessments can suit the culture of the school and the student body, and to be able delineate the graduate's profile in a manner that is specific, personal, embedded in tangible experiences, and, therefore, authentic.

It is this book's argument that the direction of travel of summative assessment at the end of high school must allow for flexibility. It must embed trust in the school's teachers and staff, to allow them to assess student work in a manner that best fits the context rather than the rigid parameters of large-scale assessment instruments. Finally, even self-assessment by students, despite the inherent problems this brings in reliability, would be a more reflective and formative approach, as in the case of portfolio assessment. To keep costs down, much of the assessment would have to be internal. Unity would be required for external validation of assessment practices: that is, educators would have to agree on the overarching construct being assessed and on the need for flexibility in reaching that construct's outcomes — which depend on the student, the school, the district, the resources, the country, and the language of instruction.

Imagine, for example, a unified acceptance of the Ecolint Learner Passport as a model of assessment, allowing teachers, mentors, and, in some instances, the students themselves to assess learning through the seven global competences. This could be done in several different languages since the language of test setters and raters would no longer be relevant. The visual representation of accumulated competences has universal currency: anyone looking at the transcript can appreciate it.

If, as this book is arguing, different schools, districts, and countries had different competence-based assessment models, only one conversion system would need to be designed to translate their different practices into something that could transfer into several different institutions' references.

2.3   The Vision for a More Inclusive World

This book is an exhortation for a more inclusive educational system in which curriculum structure, in particular assessment at the end of high school, allows every bird to fly and every star to shine.

For this to be done, the chokehold of narrow, high-stakes assessment must be broken, and a new, more holistic approach such as the Ecolint Learner Passport, opened. If enough educational institutions work together to put pressure on examination boards to change and postsecondary institutions to recognise such change — which would be in the form of accepting more alternative transcripts — this could become a reality.

For deep educational change to take place, not only is collaboration between all stakeholders key. Equally important is a strong understanding and vision of what needs to change, why it should change, and what it should be changed into. The purpose of this book is to provide this vision. Now, all of us invested in the mission of education for a better world and assessment for human flourishing must continue this work.

References

Coalition [Coalition to Honour All Learning] (2024). [Website]. Ecolint. https://sites.google.com/ecolint.ch/honour-all-learning/home

Ecolint. (2024). *Our history.* https://www.ecolint.ch/en/our-history

Hughes, C. (2020). *The Universal Learning Programme: Educating future-ready citizens.* In-Progress Reflections on Current and Critical Issues in Curriculum, Learning, and Assessment, 34. UNESCO IBE. https://unesdoc.unesco.org/ark:/48223/pf0000372613

Hughes, C. (2023). *The necessity to broaden assessment and how we can do it.* Thematic note 18. Curriculum on the Move series. UNESCO IBE. https://unesdoc.unesco.org/ark:/48223/pf0000384874

Hughes, C. (2024). *Competences.* Thematic note 18. Curriculum on the Move series. UNESCO IBE. https://www.ibe.unesco.org/en/articles/competences

Hughes, C., & Acedo, C. (2017). *Guiding principles for learning in the twenty-first century.* Educational Practices 28. UNESCO IBE & International Academy of Education (IAE). https://unesdoc.unesco.org/ark:/48223/pf0000262678

Index

About the Author

Conrad Hughes (MA, PhD, EdD) is the Director General of the International School of Geneva, the oldest international school in the world. He is also Professor in Practice at the University of Durham's School of Education. He was School Principal, Director of Education, International Baccalaureate Diploma Programme Coordinator, and teacher in schools in Switzerland, France, India, and the Netherlands.

Hughes is also a UNESCO IBE Senior Fellow, a member of the advisory board for the University of the People, and an associate researcher in the Department of Psychology and Education at the University of Geneva.

He is the author of numerous articles in peer-reviewed journals and, as Director of Education at the International School of Geneva, he led the publication of *Guiding Principles for Learning in the 21st Century* with UNESCO IBE. He was a guest editor for a special issue of *Prospects*, with entries by leading academics such as Sugata Mitra, Steve Higgins, Doug & Lynn Newton, Scilla Elworthy, Paul Black, AC Grayling and Juan Carlos Tedesco.

Hughes' most recent books are *Education and Elitism: Challenges and Opportunities* (2021, Routledge), *Educating for the 21st Century: Seven Global Challenges* (2018, Brill), and *Understanding Prejudice and Education: The Challenge for Future Generations* (2017, Routledge).

Printed in the United States
by Baker & Taylor Publisher Services